WHO DARES WINS

THE SPECIAL FORCES WAY TO CONQUER FEAR AND SUCCEED

WHO DARES WINS

THE SPECIAL FORCES WAY TO CONQUER FEAR AND SUCCEED

BOB MAYER

POCKET BOOKS

NEW YORK LONDON TORONTO SYDNEY

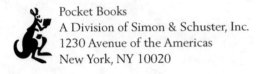 Pocket Books
A Division of Simon & Schuster, Inc.
1230 Avenue of the Americas
New York, NY 10020

First Pocket Books trade paperback edition June 2009

POCKET and colophon are registered trademarks of Simon & Schuster, Inc.

For information about special discounts for bulk purchases,
please contact Simon & Schuster Special Sales at
1-866-506-1949 or business@simonandschuster.com.

The Simon & Schuster Speakers Bureau can bring authors
to your live event. For more information or to book an event,
contact the Simon & Schuster Speakers Bureau at 1-866-248-3049
or visit our website at www.simonspeakers.com.

Designed by Ruth Lee-Mui

Manufactured in the United States of America

10 9 8 7 6 5 4 3 2 1

ISBN 978-1-4165-9308-9
ISBN 978-1-4391-0091-2 (ebook)

To all who've
served in Special Forces

De Oppresso Liber

CONTENTS

CONTENTS

INTRODUCTION

WHY SHOULD YOU READ THIS BOOK?

In tough times, it's the tough who succeed. The Green Berets are the mentally and emotionally toughest soldiers in the military. The first thing you'll sense when you meet a Green Beret is that he exudes *confidence*. It's a palpable sensation. He has confidence in himself, his team, his unit.

How did he become this way?

He changed. And that's what this book is all about. You wouldn't have picked it up if there wasn't something in your life you wanted to change. It could be something minor or it could be life-altering. This book will teach you the path to change.

There are nine tools in *Who Dares Wins*, and by learning to use them you will gain the insight and knowledge to change, in the same way Special Forces soldiers go from being regular soldiers to being the best. This book gives you a comprehensive plan to build self-confidence so you can conquer fear and succeed.

The definition of confidence is: Trust in a person or thing. A feeling of assurance.

Do you want to feel confident in all aspects of your life?

You have goals. You want to succeed. For most people, the largest obstacle to success is fear. This book brings you strategies and tactics used by the U.S. Army's Green Berets to conquer fear, to succeed, and to build confidence.

Success means different things to different people. So, in addition to the tools, you'll find examples for using them in a variety of situations. You'll learn how to customize these templates to fit your goals. You'll also get specific exercises, using each tool, that will help make your life more successful as you learn how to change.

This is a complete program for life, covering a broad spectrum, from goal-setting (*What*), to personality and growth (*Character* and *Change*), to leadership and interaction with others (*Command* and *Communication*), among others. But they all connect, with you at the very center.

But before you start, you have to ask yourself one very important question:

DO YOU WANT TO CHANGE?

It's that simple. Change is extremely difficult, for many reasons. The good news is, experts have blazed the way for you, and you can use the lessons they learned and the techniques they developed.

Do you want a life ruled by fear, or do you want to live your life to the fullest, confident in yourself?

A successful person can make decisions and take action in the face of fear. The successful are head and shoulders above their competition. They accomplish their goals, have pride in themselves, and find a way to achieve what they want in life. The successful dare to take chances and succeed.

Fear is the number one barrier that keeps you rooted in the mundane and ordinary. It is the primary obstacle to achieving your dreams. Successful people take action despite their fears. As you'll discover, it is not a question of ignoring fear, but rather the opposite: you must factor fear into your life and deal with it.

A lot of what you will learn in this book seems common sense. A lot will also be counterintuitive. We make repeated mistakes in our lives without learning from them. This book teaches you how to focus, learn from errors, and not repeat them. Since we all make mistakes, the positive news is that there are ways we can improve. We are emotional creatures, and most often our emotions overrule our common sense. Intellectually, our subconscious often overpowers our conscious. We will focus on trying to find the real reasons why we do things, which are often right in front of us but which we are blind to.

WHAT'S IN THIS BOOK?

WHO. DARES. WINS.

The book is broken down into three areas. In each are three tools, each tool simplified to one word.

The first area we'll work in is **WINS**. Why? Because it's key to know where you're going—what you want to change (goals)—first.

You have to understand **What** you want to change; **Why** you want to change; and **Where** the change will occur.

From there we will go to **WHO.** Why? Because once you know what you want to WIN, you need to understand yourself.

You have to understand what your **Character** can do, what it can't do (yet), and what your blind spot is; what **Change** is and how you accomplish it; and how to build **Courage** to change.

Finally, we will tackle **DARES.** Why? Because once you know what you want to WIN, and understand WHO you are, it's time to take risks and push yourself from ordinary to successful.

You have to **Communicate** effectively to implement your change to others; take **Command** of your change; and then **Complete** the Circle of Success, pulling all nine tools together to conquer fear and succeed.

HOW DOES *WHO DARES WINS* WORK?

Most books about personal improvement take either a scientific, practical approach or a nebulous, theoretical angle. In *Who Dares Wins* I combine two apparently unrelated approaches: the practical way Special Forces personnel train and operate, and the creativity of an artist's process.

This book is focused on the individual, but successful people are the building blocks of successful teams. So once the individual Circle of Success is completed, a *team* Circle of Success can be implemented (page xiv). Special Forces develops the world's most effective warriors and builds them into the most flexible and elite fighting unit on earth: the Special Forces A-Team. This book is the first step in building the winning A-Team. As we get further into the book, I discuss teams more and more because we are all parts of teams—whether they be family, social, or work related.

Special Operations Forces soldiers are the military's artists:

those who have honed their craft so well, they can create and achieve beyond the norm.

Immediate Action Drills (pages 187–189) are designed exactly as the words indicate: to allow immediate responses to problems. They are succinct summaries of concepts and actions to be taken for each tool. And I show you how the tools applied as I wrote this book.

Here's what you'll see in every tool:

- Introduction—an overview of the tool
- A blood lesson example to highlight the importance of the tool
- A step-by-step description that breaks the tool down into usable templates
- Exercises to help you implement the templates in your life
- An artist's imagination example of how the tool works in the creative world of writing

WHAT ARE BLOOD LESSONS?

I use blood lessons as teaching tools, the same way the U.S. Army Special Forces, the Green Berets, do. These are the most successful, flexible fighting soldiers in the world. Their list of successes is long. Person for person, they have earned more military awards, won more battles, and influenced our nation's foreign policy far more than any other military organization. But sometimes it's the lessons learned from failures that are the most touching and enlightening.

What most people don't realize is that the Green Berets achieve as much, if not more, in peacetime as they do during war.

They are not Rambos—they're teachers. This book is your personal window into their world, and how they achieve what they do. Learn from them, and apply what you learn to your world.

I use historical examples, because blood lessons are so poignant. At times they might seem so much larger than day-to-day life, but I've picked dramatic examples so that they stay with you.

The tactics, theories, and practices in this book were not developed on Wall Street, invented by a think tank, imagined in a university ivory tower, hammered out at the club over cocktails, or theorized in a corporate boardroom. They were forged in blood across the spectrum of time, on battlefields around the world.

WHAT'S THE CIRCLE OF SUCCESS?

The nine *Who Dares Wins* tools form a Circle of Success. Each tool connects with all the others at the center, where you stand,

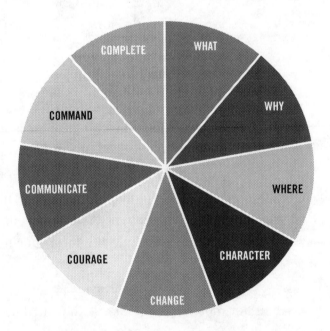

creating a clear path to follow to accomplish your life goals. When you reach the last tool in this book, you should circle right back to the first, and you'll find that your answers to the exercises you've already completed have changed based on what you've learned on your path. You stand at the center of the Circle as the linchpin that connects all the tools.

HOW ARE YOU FEELING SO FAR?

Take a deep breath.

For those of you worried this is going to be a hard-core, do-or-die military book that will have you doing push-ups in the rain, relax. I'm combining the warrior's spirit with the artist's imagination, because I've used both in my life and have found a way to mesh them into a unique path that I invite you to travel with me.

I took *Who Dares Wins* concepts, ventured into the creative world of fiction writing, and published over fifty books. Eventually, I ended up co-writing with romantic comedy writer Jenny Crusie. Our romantic adventure novels are the unlikely production of, as Jenny puts it, "a grim, paranoid, Green Beret thriller writer" collaborating with a romantic comedy writer. But the collaboration worked well enough, and our books consistently hit the *New York Times, Wall Street Journal,* and *Publishers Weekly* best-seller lists, among others. If *Who Dares Wins* could work for me in this dynamic situation, it can work for you, no matter your particular path.

I've made the process as simple as possible, but I do warn you that simple doesn't mean easy. As you will see in Tool Five: Change, just reading this book isn't going to be enough. *Who*

Dares Wins is full of moments of enlightenment, the first of the three steps of change. But change is about more than moments.

Your decisions to change and then commit to sustained actions will begin a difficult but rewarding path, a successful circle you'll build on for the rest of your life.

WHY SHOULD YOU LISTEN TO ME?

Because I've learned, practiced, and taught these techniques for decades. Because I used them to write this book and successfully run a business based on bringing these tools to the civilian world for individual confidence development, team-building, and leadership. Because it works.

I have opinions. If they make you angry or bother you, you'll have to ask yourself why you're having such a strong reaction. I've found that the things that upset me the most do so because they strike closest to home. Our greatest emotional defenses are built around our greatest personal weaknesses (our blind spots), and that makes sense in a strange sort of way. Special Operations training is often brutal and difficult, so it will break through strong emotional defenses and unveil the true character underneath. Once that happens, change can occur.

In the same way, the thing we are most afraid of is often exactly the way we are living our life—we're just not aware we're living our fears. We'll discuss this in more detail when we talk about character. The two hats I wear—Green Beret and writer—both require the study of human nature and personal interaction. Even an institution as tradition-bound as the U.S. Military Academy at West Point (founded as an engineering school, because at the time these were the skills a military leader was thought to need) has changed its focus over the course of the past century. Greater and greater emphasis is now placed on the humanities, particularly psychology. Interestingly enough, the psychology department at the Academy is called the Department of Behavioral Science and *Leadership*. For a school whose primary goal is to train leaders, it would seem significant that the psychology department is the one best suited to do that.

I throw a lot of information at you in this book. I liken reading *Who Dares Wins* to trying to take a drink from a fire hydrant. You'll quench your thirst, but there will be a lot coming at you, probably more than you can handle in one gulp. That's fine. The book's not going anywhere. You can pick it up any time you want and go back to it.

I don't suggest reading *Who Dares Wins* in one sitting. If you do, you won't be able to put the kind of thought you'll want to into the exercises. Change takes three steps. Read this book one Tool at a time. I'll make you one guarantee if you do:

You will find at least one thing in this book that you can immediately use to make your life better.

TAKE THE CHALLENGE

INTRODUCTION

Green Berets thrive on challenges. They're triple volunteers: volunteering for the Army, volunteering to become airborne qualified, and volunteering for Special Forces training. No one makes them volunteer. No one is going to make you do anything in this book. It's your challenge. This book will help you take your challenge, change, and succeed.

The key to taking the challenge is to face your fear.

Fear drives most of our lives and keeps us from living to our fullest potential. It is the most difficult thing we have to deal with and the most necessary thing to overcome in order to change and be successful. You can't ignore fear, suppress it, or let it debilitate you. You must face it, factor it into your life, and then conquer it using the tools you'll gain from reading this book.

WHAT DO YOU FEAR?

As you read this book, you'll be challenged to examine your life:

What wakes you in the middle of the night and causes you to stare out into the darkness with a gnawing feeling deep inside?

What task do you put off and avoid doing as long as possible?

What is the one thing in your life you least *want* to do, but know you *should* do?

What is the one thing in your life you most want to do, but have been afraid to try?

Which people do you least want to interact with, but know you should?

Which decision do you know you should make and implement, but lack the personal leadership to make the commitment to do?

What course of action would you like to pursue, but you fear people around you will disapprove or even actively try to stop you from doing?

Exercise 1: TAKE THE CHALLENGE

Record the one thing you fear the most. (The fear in your head is not in the real world. Writing down your fear externalizes it, so you can take action to conquer it in the real world.)

The successful take action in the face of fear. *Who Dares Wins* is the motto of the British Special Air Service, Britain's elite Special Operations Force, and nine other elite special operations forces around the world, so there must be something to it that the members of these units like. The U.S. Special Forces and Delta

Force base much of their operational templates, training, and assessment and selection of personnel on the lessons learned by the British Special Air Service.

To succeed beyond the norm, you have to be daring. Take risks. When you do, using the proper preparation and the tools illustrated in this book, you will change and succeed.

WHAT'S YOUR PRIMARY MOTIVATOR?

To be successful at facing fear, you have to understand what motivates you. Understanding this is just as important as understanding your reaction to fear.

What keeps you going, even when everything seems to be going wrong?

What pushes back the darkness in your life and makes you feel positive?

What thoughts and feelings do you draw on in order to do tasks you dread doing?

What is the *one* thing you would fight to the death to defend?

What person do you most respect and why?

Exercise 2: TAKE THE CHALLENGE

Record the one thing that motivates you the most.

Look at the conflict between your fear in Exercise 1 and motivation in Exercise 2. That conflict can make success a struggle, a battle—except that your primary enemy is inside you.

If you spend your life battling yourself, wasting energy that could be used to make your reality better, the majority of your time will be spent reacting to your fears and nightmares, not working toward the success you dream about.

Remember, it takes as much energy to be average as to be successful. It's just a question of where the energy is directed. This book will teach you to take the energy you spend battling yourself, reacting, and being in crisis, and redirect it into positive change and success.

It is said that most truths are paradoxes. *Who Dares Wins* is a set of successful techniques, ideas, and examples that will take you on your own unique path. Don't allow anything you read here to stifle *your* creativity. Your dreams are the key to your own success.

If you were a painter, *Who Dares Wins* would be your primer on understanding paint, canvas, lighting, and perspective, on how to sell your work to a gallery, and so on. But as an artist, you would ultimately be the one who has to decide *what* you want to paint and *how* to paint it. You are unique. Your life, job, family, and situation are unique. What you want to change is special to you. How you define success is something only you know. Adjust these templates to yourself. Let the creativity boiling inside of you escape and take you and those around you to higher levels.

You must first master the craft of being successful, as any artist or warrior must master the basics of his or her particular discipline. But then, allow your brilliance to lead you as you tailor *Who Dares Wins* techniques to overcoming your fears. Be original. Be a creative force in your own life. That is why at the end of this book I talk about breaking rules and taking risks under DARES.

Green Berets and artists blaze new paths, innovating strategies and tactics as they go. So can you.

YOUR PATH IS ABOUT CHANGING *YOU* AND DEVELOPING CONFIDENCE

Remember, successful people don't do things the "right" way. They do things the *brave* way. Be brave enough to accept that you don't already know all you need to know—that if you are not already where you want to be, then *you* must change in order to get somewhere else. Expect the world or other people to change in order to accommodate you, and you're in for a long wait.

The only person you can change is you—and paradoxically, that change will often bring about the results you want from others. Understand this basic truth and you are already well ahead of the pack.

How does it feel when you are around someone who exudes confidence? Don't you admire that trait? Self-confidence is critical in every aspect of your life, yet most people struggle to find it. That struggle can then cause a further loss of confidence in a spiral of defeat.

Self-confidence can be learned. As you go through the tools in this book, you'll learn where and why you lack confidence and then be given techniques to build it. This book will help you go from the left column to the right column:

LOW CONFIDENCE	HIGH CONFIDENCE
Hiding or ignoring mistakes.	Admitting mistakes and learning from them.
Doing what other people think you should.	Doing what you know is right, no matter what others say.
Letting fear dictate your actions.	Using courage to overcome fear.
Staying in your status quo, no matter how miserable you are.	Taking risks and making changes, despite the difficulty.

(*continued on next page*)

LOW CONFIDENCE	HIGH CONFIDENCE
Letting others always take charge even when you know better.	Taking charge when you are the best qualified to do so.
Letting each day happen, rather than having any purpose, plan, or goals.	Having goals, a plan, and setting out on a path to reach those goals every day.

The following Special Forces truths as applied to you will be important to remember as you embark on your creative path to success.

SPECIAL FORCES TRUTH . . .	*WHO DARES WINS* TRANSLATION . . .
Humans are more important than hardware.	You are more important than the things you have around you.
Quality is better than quantity.	Doing a few things well is better than doing many things at a mediocre level.
Special Operations Forces can't be mass-produced.	Only five percent of people rise to the status of successful.
Special Operations Forces can't be created after emergencies occur.	Preparing can prevent most emergencies, and help you handle the ones that do occur.

AREA ONE

WINS

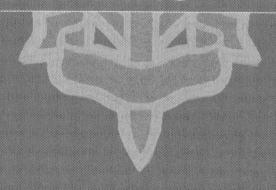

You must have goals that are clearly defined and
can be stated in one sentence.

You must understand why you're trying to achieve your goals,
what impact they'll have on your environment, and
how your environment affects you.

"Generally in battle, use the normal force to engage; use the extraordinary to win."

—SUN TZU

We'll cover the *Wins* part of *Who Dares Wins* first, because it's best to have a clear direction as you work through the next two areas. Using *Who Dares Wins* techniques, you'll begin by specifying goals, then understanding why you want to achieve them, and finish by studying the situation in which you are trying to have success.

We will work on *What* (goals) you want to change. Then examine *Why* (intent) you want to change and achieve your goals. Then study *Where* (environment) change will occur.

Goals are future oriented. Planning for the future is a cornerstone of Special Forces. A successful individual acts, while those that make up the norm are trying to maintain the status quo. Most people do not have well-defined, clear goals and thus never change. They spend significant time reacting instead of acting. Trying to achieve a goal through reaction is a self-defeating approach: you're allowing your efforts to be dictated by external forces and others' goals. To avoid this, it's important that you apply the three tools in this area to your life, then you'll be on the path to succeed the Green Beret way.

WHAT DO YOU WANT TO CHANGE AND ACHIEVE?

INTRODUCTION

> "If you don't know where you are going, you are liable to end
> up somewhere else."
>
> —CASEY STENGEL

The *one-sentence goal* is the tool that will become the foundation
of everything you do. Having an idea of where you're going, before you start on your path, is a key tenet of Green Beret operations. Then, being aware of the priority of goals and aligning the
hierarchy can reduce conflict and enhance success.

**Clearly understanding your goals keeps you on target to
succeed.**

SPECIAL FORCES ASSESSMENT AND SELECTION THOUGHT:
Take your eyes off the price and put them on the prize.

BLOOD LESSON: THE MAN WHO NEVER WAS

> "Enterprises must be prepared, with specially trained troops of
> the hunter class, who can develop a reign of terror, leaving a
> trail of German corpses behind them."
>
> —WINSTON CHURCHILL

Let's look at a *What* for a complex, large-scale military problem that was successfully solved, beginning with a one-sentence goal.

The problem

In 1943, the Allies were poised to invade Europe after successfully invading North Africa. The next obvious place to attack was Sicily. To quote Churchill, "Anyone but a fool would realize it's Sicily."

There was a very big problem: **how to stop the Germans from massing their forces in Sicily and defeating the invasion.**

Solving this problem was tasked to an officer in MI5, the forerunner of the British Security Service. Lieutenant Commander Ewen Montagu decided the British needed to give the Germans solid evidence that the attack would occur elsewhere. Evidence that they would believe.

He boiled this complex problem down to this one-sentence *What:*

I will implement a plan to convince the Germans the attack is coming someplace other than Sicily long enough before the actual invasion to influence the German reaction.

The solution

This simple, one-sentence "*What* do I want to achieve?" led to a very complex plan to solve the problem:

Montagu found a corpse—a homeless man who had died of pneumonia after ingesting rat poison. During an autopsy, such a death would appear very similar to that of a person who'd drowned.

He created a military persona for the man—a complete identity, down to the smallest detail. The homeless corpse became Captain/Acting Major William Martin, Royal Marine.

Montagu went so far as to place theater stubs in Martin's pockets along with love letters from his "fiancée," a clerk in Montagu's office. In a briefcase chained to Major Martin's body, certain key documents were placed, all fakes: letters between generals discussing a dual attack on Sardinia and Corsica and on Greece. The letters said a deception plan was being implemented to fool the Germans into thinking the attack would really take place against Sicily.

The body, packed in ice, was put in a canister, placed aboard a British submarine, and sailed to a point off the Spanish coast. The submarine surfaced, the body was unpacked, a life jacket was placed around it, and it was cast into the ocean. The body was found by a Spanish fisherman the next day, and the documents eventually wound up in the hands of German agents. The body was turned over to the British consulate a few days later, sans briefcase. The British demanded the return of the documents, and the Spanish government complied. Examining them, the British discovered that they had been surreptitiously opened. The fake evidence had been read by the Germans.

With what results?

Hitler was so convinced of the authenticity of the documents that he ignored the logical idea that Sicily was the site of the next Allied attack. The Germans deployed forces to Sardinia, Corsica, and Greece. They also redeployed two Panzer divisions from the Russian front to Greece under the command of Field Marshal Rommel, weakening themselves in an area even Montagu couldn't have anticipated.

The lesson

Montagu's clear understanding of the *What* of his mission paid off in dividends that changed the course of World War II even beyond the invasion of Sicily. During the invasion of Normandy, when the Germans captured *real* top-secret documents from an abandoned landing craft showing future Allied operations, Hitler refused to believe them, feeling they were another setup, even though they were real.

All this, from one simple *What*.

STATE YOUR GOALS IN ONE SENTENCE

For now, we'll focus on learning how to state goals in one sentence rather than on what the goals themselves are.

Here's what you're looking for in your sentence:

- A positive verb that indicates the action that you want to achieve.
- A verb that indicates an action you control.
- Concise, understandable wording.
- An external, visible outcome.
- A time lock for accomplishing the goal, if applicable.

KEEP IT POSITIVE.
A NEGATIVE GOAL ACCEPTS DEFEAT.

A boxer with the goal "Not to get my head beaten off" is already down for the count. If you want to lose weight, avoid saying, "I don't want to be overweight." Where's the action? Perhaps what you mean instead is, "I want to work out for a minimum of thirty minutes each day to be physically fit." Then add a second goal: "I want to carefully watch what I eat and only consume healthy foods."

Don't define your goals in terms of whatever crisis you fear may be coming toward you. We'll plan for possible catastrophes later. It's enough for now to figure out a positive, understandable, external *What*. This clearly defined goal will keep you on your Circle of Success path when you're enmeshed in working with the other eight tools.

Most people spend their lives in crisis, overly focused on obstacles and fears, with no clear goal in mind. Thus they never change. A successful person must rise above crisis mode and continue to move toward his or her goals. When people do that, they begin to change.

In Special Forces, the mission statement drives everything else. The mission statement is the Green Beret's *What*. Each team is assigned specific goals. Each person on the team is also assigned specific goals that, when achieved, lead to mission success.

To live a successful life, you must clearly state *all* of your goals, both personal and professional.

Many people view their lives as a series of complex problems that require complex solutions, and they quickly become overwhelmed. But what if they narrowed their goals down to a simple, attainable series of *What* sentences?

To define your goals, you need to ask yourself several key questions regarding whatever it is you want to achieve:

- Did anyone else achieve this goal? It is most likely you won't be the first person to attempt this.

- What do you fear doing? Our greatest inhibitor to achieving our goals is usually a blind spot. Successful people walk directly into what they fear the most and conquer it.
- Why did other people do it?
- How will you know when you have achieved your goal?
- What will be the external, visible result?
- How did others define it?
- How long did it take other people to achieve the goal?

Here is a simple example taken from the Green Berets, using these key questions:

THE GOAL: A Special Forces candidate will complete the twelve-mile forced march, carrying 55 pounds of equipment, in under three hours.

Why should anyone want to achieve this goal? It's been a standard for years. And there is a reason for the standard, as Special Forces soldiers spend a great deal of time making long overland movements with much heavier loads than this. The only person I ever had removed from my team was removed because he could not keep up on our overland movements under heavy loads.

What do you fear doing? Leading up to this twelve-mile march, candidates are tested at marching various distances without knowing what the time standard is. This forces them to make decisions that could determine whether or not they succeed, going directly at their greatest fear, that of failing the course.

Why did other people do it? Throughout history, soldiers have ultimately had to rely on their feet to get them where they're going. Even in modern warfare, boots on the ground still make the final difference.

How will you know when you have achieved your goal? What will be the external, visible result? You'll have completed the march in under three hours.

How did others define it? Twelve miles, three hours, varied terrain: that's the standard for the Expert Infantryman Badge.

PRIMARY GOALS

The successful person acts. The fearful person reacts. To act in the face of fear, you'll need primary goals. Everything else, especially subordinate goals, is built upon them. Your primary goals dictate the direction of your Circle of Success. If they change at any point on your path, you should actually find yourself redefining them and working through on an entirely different circle.

You might know your primary goals right now, but if you don't, it's not a problem. We're going to cover this in more depth when we get to Tool Four: Character, and Tool Six: Courage. Everything else in your Circle of Success can change as you innovate, but your primary goals are your solid, immovable base.

For example, for the Green Beret goal, the candidate has to complete the twelve-mile rucksack march in less than three hours. That is subordinate to the goal of successfully passing the Special Forces Qualification Course. Both of these goals are subordinate to the primary goal of becoming a Special Forces soldier. Everything that a candidate does is based on the primary goal.

For example, if your goal is to become physically fit (a positive way to say "to lose weight"), then your eating habits and your physical activities both have to support that goal. Also, your family has to support this goal in terms of your diet, which may be different from your normal family meals.

The *Who Dares Wins* technique of one-sentence goal defining can work on the spectrum from primary, life-changing goals to short-lived decision-making goals.

It's important to write your goals down, so you can make sure every word means something. For the purpose of this exercise, start small.

For example:

I will write four thousand words this week for my new novel.

Exercise 3: WHAT

In one sentence, write down a short-term goal that you want to achieve this week.

Does the sentence make sense? Does each word mean something? Is the verb a positive action? Is there an external, visible outcome so you can judge whether you've achieved your goal? Do you have a time lock to achieve it within the next week?

Remember, Montagu's *What* wasn't "Stop the Germans from believing the invasion would come in Sicily." His positive goal led him to take an action, and his solution *made* the Germans think something else.

Once you write your primary goals down, you have a great degree of latitude in deciding how you want to achieve them. But first you must make sure you have a clear goal to work with.

SUBORDINATE GOALS AND ALIGNMENT

Underneath each primary goal, there are subordinate goals. At the end of this book, when you develop your complete plan for your

Circle of Success, make sure your subordinate goals support the primary goal. Also make sure that subordinate goals don't conflict.

"Success demands singleness of purpose."

—VINCE LOMBARDI

After writing down your primary goal, you must identify the subordinate goals that are part of achieving your primary goal. Consider these goal categories:

- Relationship
- Financial
- Professional
- Hobby
- Physical
- Academic
- Family

Why so many goals in so many different areas? Because, as much as possible, your subordinate goals must align with one another and your primary goals. Competing goals create conflict, causing you to waste a lot of energy trying to balance your actions.

Goals within a military chain of command, just like goals in your life, are intertwined with one another. Each level of goals depends on the one above it for direction, and the one below it for execution. Here is an example from Special Forces:

1. *Organizational Goal:* Special Forces will be prepared to conduct the six Special Operations Forces missions of Unconventional Warfare, Direct Action, Strategic Reconnaissance, Foreign Internal Defense, Counterterrorism, and Coalition Warfare/Support.

2. *A-Team Goal:* Team 055 will be prepared to conduct all above missions with an emphasis on Strategic Reconnaissance with maritime operations capability.
3. *Mission Goal:* Team 055 will infiltrate Operational Area Claw to conduct Strategic Reconnaissance along the designated sector of rail line for fourteen days, reporting movement of battalion level and higher units.
4. *Individual Goals:* Senior Communications Sergeant will maintain a secure link with higher headquarters. Senior Communications Sergeant will report all designated traffic along rail line to higher headquarters four times daily.

Note that all these goals are in alignment. Conflict occurs when goals do not align.

WHAT: AN A-TEAM EXPERIENCE

When I was an A-Team leader, the battalion operations officer told me to have my team set up a combination land navigation course and rifle range for the entire battalion. He said the commander wanted the men to go through a strenuous overland movement and finish at the rifle range, where they would qualify on their weapons.

I asked the operations officer what the primary goal of the exercise was. Was it to qualify on weapons or to practice land navigation?

His response was that the battalion commander, our boss, wanted the men to go through a "gut check." Which was neither of the above.

So, there were a few problems.

I was told to do three things: land navigation, rifle range, gut check. All could be part of one exercise, but what I really needed to know, and what I hadn't been told, was the primary goal of the training I was to plan. While this might not have seemed an issue initially—after all, it appears all I had to do was set up a land navigation course ending at a rifle range—as you will soon see, it was a major problem.

I went back to my team room and did a rather strange thing. I pulled out the Army field manual for conducting training, blew the dust off it, and read the chapters on how to plan training. I made some notes, went back to the battalion operations officer, and told him that according to the field manual, the primary goal of the training needed to be specified before planning could proceed. He needed to tell me in one sentence the *What*.

Was I greeted with open arms and a hearty slap on the back for following approved Army procedure?

As you can guess, of course not. After some choice words ending with "You're just a captain, and you do what the battalion commander wants!" I was tossed out of the office.

So, did I smarten up and leave it at that?

Of course not. There were too many questions:

1. Was the land navigation important?
2. Was the goal of the land navigation simply to make the men cover a certain amount of distance before arriving at the firing range, so that they would fire under simulated combat conditions? If so, I could accomplish the same thing in a much more straightforward manner by simply having the men do a forced march to the rifle range and save time and effort all around.
3. Was this to be our required annual qualification? If so, then the

firing was preeminent, as this was a test each soldier had to pass. In that case, a forced march would be detrimental, but a relatively easy land navigation course would not be a problem.

4. Was the cross-country movement to be done tactically? Would the men carry full rucksacks?

5. What exactly did the commander mean by "gut check"?

Notice the number of questions generated when the primary *What* isn't clear and the *Why* isn't stated.

Eventually word of this got to the commander. He stopped by my team room and asked me what the problem was. I explained that I could easily plan and conduct this training, but it would be helpful if I knew *what* his primary goal was and *why* he wanted to do it. He explained his goal: "I want the men pushed to their limits within the designated time period, both mentally and physically [*What*], to test individual fortitude and team cohesion [*Why*]."

This goal was very different from that of designing a land navigation course and a rifle range.

What we ended up with was the Gut Check.

1. We started with a no-notice alert, bringing the team in.

2. We had them pack up and head out to the airfield, rig for jumping, board an aircraft, and conduct a parachute infiltration.

3. They were met on the drop zone by an "agent" who gave them coordinates for their next point.

4. If they made the next point in time, they found food and directions; if they didn't make it in time, they found just the directions to the next point.

5. And so on until the team covered an extensive amount of ground in a specified time period.

Few teams made it through the Gut Check successfully. We found it tested team cohesion quite well and challenged individual fortitude, thus fulfilling the commander's primary goal.

The rifle range portion was dropped for logistical reasons. It was something the operations officer had tacked on (for his own reasons—*Why*), thinking it would be a nice addition. In reality it would have forced planning to go in an entirely different direction. It would have changed the required environment—*Where*—for the exercise and would not have achieved what the commander desired.

I was able to give the commander exactly what he wanted, based on just that one sentence of instructions detailing his intent, which is why Tool Two, *Why*, is so important and comes next.

WHAT: THE ARTIST'S IMAGINATION

I spend the entire first day of my writers workshop having students write a single sentence: the *What* for their book. Being able to say what their book is about in that one sentence helps them focus their book idea. I have found in my study of the creative writing process that the original vision (*What*) for a story often gets lost while a novel is being written. Likewise, you can also lose sight of what drives you when you try to change. I spend a large amount of time at the beginning of my *Who Dares Wins* workshops having people write down their *What*'s (goals) and analyzing them to make sure they are really the goals they want.

An author has to write down the original idea that starts his creative process before he can come up with a story. Every creative idea has been written about before, and pretty much every goal has been tried. The difference in your life will be how you follow up on your goals. That's where your creativity will thrive. That's where your positive emotional energy has to drive you.

Write down your goals and post them where you can see them every day, so that you stay on the same path every day. For a book, I tell writers to post their one-sentence original idea (*What*) someplace where they see it every day when they begin writing. As with any other goal, it's the one part of the book that can't change without forcing everything else in the Circle of Success to change. It keeps the author focused, allowing the big picture to be clearly seen in one sentence. It's easy to get lost in the forest of a 400-page manuscript. Beyond the writing of the book, like Montagu's *What* serving purposes beyond the immediate one, the one-sentence *What* for a book is often the core of the pitch to sell the book, to the agent, to the editor, to the publisher, to the sales force, to the bookstore buyer, to the reader.

Exercise 4: WHAT

Divide a piece of lined paper into four equal columns.

Label each column: *What, Why, Where, Done.*

Under the first column, *What*, write a subordinate goal for each of the areas that apply in which you want to achieve a goal in the next week (nothing major, just a basic, simple goal).

The areas can be: Academic, Physical, Family, Relationship, Hobby, Spiritual, Professional, Task, Financial, etc.

WHY DO YOU WANT TO CHANGE
AND TO ACHIEVE YOUR GOALS?

INTRODUCTION

"He who has a why to live can bear with almost any how."

—NIETZSCHE

Understanding *why* you want to change and achieve your goals improves your morale and motivation. It allows you to utilize your initiative and expertise to achieve and succeed. Sometimes, understanding *why* you want to achieve something will change the *What*, as you saw in the A-Team example in the previous tool.

SPECIAL FORCES ASSESSMENT AND SELECTION THOUGHT:
Positive thoughts bring positive results.

BLOOD LESSON: THE BEST DEFENSE IS TO TAKE ACTION

The first American Special Operations Force was Rogers' Rangers. Robert Rogers was a colonial farmer from New Hampshire, recruited by the British in 1755 to serve in the French and Indian War. Over the course of the following years he formed a unit of colonials called Rogers' Rangers, the first Ranger unit.

Unlike the British regulars, they wore green uniforms and utilized unconventional tactics, many of which were written down as

Rogers' Rules of Ranging, some of which are still used in the current U.S. Army Ranger Handbook.

The problem

The most significant engagement the Rangers fought was with the Abenaki Indians in Canada. This tribe had been raiding the colonies and was credited during the war with over five hundred kills, mostly of civilians.

Rogers's assigned *What* was "Stop the Abenaki."

Notice this was phrased in the negative, and it was a reaction. Rogers saw the problem with that goal.

Conventional wisdom at the time dictated a defensive posture along the frontier. Rogers realized that would leave the initiative in the hands of his enemies.

The solution

Rogers had to ask himself *why* they needed to stop the Abenaki: to stop the raids and the killings. Rogers knew the frontier was simply too large to be adequately defended with the scant forces he had. Looking at his *Why* changed his *What*.

He decided that the only way to stop the scourge was to go to the source. He had to switch from conventional tactics to unconventional ones. Others told him that was impossible because it would require his Rangers to venture too far inside enemy territory and would leave the frontier undefended. It would mean taking too great a risk—being too daring.

Rogers figured that the other side was thinking that way, too, and this would increase his odds of success.

He changed the reactive, fearful verb of the *What* into a positive action:

I will lead my Rangers to attack and destroy the Abenaki.

His reasoning? If no one considered the raid a real possibility, the enemy wouldn't be prepared to defend against it. It was a risk worth taking.

A successful individual finds new ways to tackle problems, and is willing to take risks to succeed. He is willing to change the status quo.

The lesson

Leading a Ranger force of two hundred men, Rogers marched into Canada and destroyed the Abenaki village, a feat shown in the 1940 movie *Northwest Passage*, starring Spencer Tracy. This was a case of thinking outside of the normal parameters on Rogers's part.

KNOW YOUR *WHY* (INTENT)

For every *What* (goal) you have, you need a *Why* (intent). A goal is usually factual and external, while your *Why*'s are emotional and internal.

Any time you develop a *What*, you are establishing a *Why* at the same time.

When you want to change something, there is always a reason *why* you want to change.

For many people, the *Why* remains buried in their subconscious and does them little good. It is critical not only to keep your *Why* in your conscious mind, but to write it down to make it real.

The *Why* (intent) and *What* (goal) should be mutually

supportive. Like the goal, the intent should be a positive statement, because we want positive emotions.

When you state your goal's intent, follow this format:

I am doing X (*What*) for reason Y (*Why*).

When I first entered the Army, the key portion of the operations order was the mission statement, which detailed *What* the unit and members were to accomplish. About five years later, someone came up with the idea of adding the Commander's Intent to the mission statement. This considerably improved the effectiveness of an operations order. Since you are the commander of your life (Tool Eight: Command), you must know your intent.

Like the goal, the intent should be stated positively. Remember, you will respond better to positive emotions than to negative ones.

EXAMPLES OF BAD INTENTS INCLUDE:
- Because the boss said so.
- So I don't get fired.
- So I don't go bankrupt.
- So my spouse doesn't leave me.
- So I don't have a heart attack from being overweight.
- Because I can't stop myself.
- Because it seems like fun.
- So I look busy.
- So I don't lose my home.

EXAMPLES OF GOOD INTENTS INCLUDE:
- Because it saves me time.
- So I can do my job more efficiently and get promoted.

- Because I will be physically fit and feel better, emotionally and physically.
- Because it will reduce my anxiety over money and allow me to focus that energy on other things.
- Because it will improve my relationship with my spouse.
- Because it *is* fun.
- Because it is a dream I've always wanted to achieve.

Because intent gives direction but not specific instructions, it allows a large degree of latitude as you further develop your goals and decide how you are going to achieve them. Intent helps you innovate and motivate. Intent is a critical element of Special Forces operations planning because it allows these highly trained men to use their skills and creativity to maximum effect.

But how do you innovate?

Try the following processes:

1. *Ask yourself: What if?* Project out courses of actions, much like a chess master, trying to see how they will play out. Enlist the aid of others in doing this. In particular, focus on suggestions that you have a strong initial negative reaction to. Our greatest weaknesses have our greatest emotional defenses built around them, and that extends to *What* and *Why*.

2. *Study and research.* You are not the first one to face whatever challenge it is that's ahead of you. Study how others overcame it. We'll discuss this more in the next tool when we cover the Special Forces area study (page 37).

3. *Take it one step further.* Yes, maybe you can achieve your goal by doing A. But what about if you go beyond A? What if what appears

to be isn't what it appears to be? Note the example of "The Woman Who Was" (page 158).

4. *Reverse your thinking.* Stop beating your head against the wall. Back off, walk around the wall, and look at it from the other side. Change your perspective and stop having tunnel vision.

5. *What if you're wrong?* What if your blind spot is controlling you? (We'll cover this in Tool Four: Character.) Sometimes, if things don't feel right, you need to stop and pay attention to those feelings. As a writer, I'm not a big fan of the concept of writer's block—I usually call it laziness. However, if for several days in a row I feel disquiet about what I'm writing, I take that as a warning that I'm going in the wrong direction. At times like that I put the brakes on and step back from what I'm working on. I drop my preconceived notions.

6. *Keep it simple.* This seems to contradict some of the earlier techniques, such as *Take it one step further.* However, when you are doing something completely new to you, it is often best to keep things as simple as possible so that you can focus on the goal and not get bogged down in the process.

Clear intent helps you stay consistently motivated. When you use your initiative, your morale inevitably goes up.

DESIGN BOUNDARIES USING YOUR *WHY*

While intent (*Why*) should be stated positively, you have to be clear about your limits as you define each goal and what you want to change. Successful people should not need much external motivation, but they do need clearly drawn boundaries. You can take any change to an unhealthy extreme.

The key to setting limits is to avoid unexpected, and undesired, results. For example, in Ranger School, the instructors are insistent that the students take action immediately.

The *Why* (intent) behind this? In an ambush situation you don't have time to think—you have to act, and often in a way that is contrary to common sense. The proper reaction to being ambushed is to assault *into* the ambushing force.

One day a group of Ranger School students were being bussed to a training site. When the bus stopped, an instructor jumped on board screaming at the students to get off the bus NOW! The students took action. They kicked out the windows and poured out of the bus. Needless to say, they achieved the *What* the instructors were looking for, but not exactly in a way that was appreciated by the chain of command.

If your goal is to become physically fit, you need to know what your limits are, because going too far can be dangerous and you can end up hurting yourself, negating your goal and the change. Pretty much anything taken to an extreme can be dangerous. We'll discuss this more in Tool Four: Character.

Exercise 5: WHY

Using the four-column sheet from Exercise 4, fill out the second column. Next to each *What*, list the *Why* in the second column. I am doing X (*What*) for reason Y (*Why*).

Examine your results. Do you have a positive *Why*?
Are some of your *Why*'s reactive?
Are some of your *Why*'s based on fear?
For each *What* that has a negative *Why*, rewrite the *Why* to be positive—or consider redefining the *What* or dropping it.

WHY: THE ARTIST'S IMAGINATION

After deciding *what* someone wants to write a book about, I then ask them *why* they want to write about it. What effect do they wish to achieve? The same story told two slightly different ways will have a very different impact.

The *Why* makes the *What* exciting, because it allows for a variety of approaches. Every *What* has been done—every idea has already been told. But every *Why* hasn't. Being able to give the *Why* for a book means the author understands the intent he or she wants to transmit to readers. They know what emotion they want the reader to walk away with.

They also have a better understanding of their own motivation for writing the book. Sometimes, they realize that their *What* is wrong because it won't achieve their *Why*. Then they end up adjusting the *What* so that it is in line with their intent.

TOOL THREE

WHERE WILL CHANGE OCCUR?

INTRODUCTION

"By terrain I mean distances, whether the ground is traversed with ease or difficulty, whether it is open or constricted, and the chances of life or death."

—SUN TZU

Understanding your environment helps you work in harmony with it and those around you. In this tool, you'll use the Special Forces Area Study to understand your environment's effect on you and your effect on your environment: *Where*.

SPECIAL FORCES ASSESSMENT AND SELECTION THOUGHT:
Difficulties are meant to rouse, not discourage.

BLOOD LESSON: LEARNING THE HARD WAY— THE ORIGIN OF THE SEALS

The Special Forces team I commanded had the additional specialty of being a maritime operations team. We spent a lot of time in the water, including attending the Royal Danish Navy's Fromandkorpset (Frogman Corps) combat swim school in Denmark. We learned the importance of reconnaissance and hydrographic studies. The Marine Corps in World War II learned the importance of such studies during the Tarawa campaign.

The problem

In 1943 the United States was going on the offensive in the
Pacific. One of the objectives was the Marshall Islands, which
would serve as air bases to further the advance toward Japan. But
before they could take the Marshalls, the Americans had to take
the Gilberts, which lay in the way and had one operational air
base on Betio, part of the atoll called Tarawa.

The commander of the Japanese forces defending Tarawa,
Admiral Shibasaki, was so confident of his defenses that he pro-
claimed that "a million men cannot take Tarawa in a hundred
years." On an island only a mile long and a few hundred yards
wide, he had twenty-six hundred elite Imperial Marines, fourteen
coastal defense guns, forty dug-in artillery pieces, and over one
hundred well-emplaced machine guns with interlocking fields of
fire. The defenders had a four-foot-high log seawall covering all
approaches to shore.

On the opposite side, the American naval commander (note
that it was the Navy commander, not the Marine commander) felt
equally confident about taking Tarawa: "We will destroy it," he
said. "We will obliterate it."

This brings to mind one of my team sergeant's standing operating procedures: "Nothing is impossible to the man who doesn't
have to do it."

The American admiral had reason to be confident: the task
force approaching Tarawa consisted of seventeen aircraft carriers,
twelve battleships, and numerous support ships, along with the
Second Marine Division and part of the Army's Thirty-seventh
Division, all told about 35,000 fighting men.

The admiral had a clear understanding of his *What* (goal: take the island) and his *Why* (intent: to control the air base) but he had not studied his *Where:* Tarawa.

The solution

At 0215 on 20 November 1943, the Marines offshore went to general quarters. They received last rites (someone had great yet depressing foresight) and boarded their landing craft. At 0505 the naval bombardment of Tarawa began. The only times the bombardment paused were to allow dive bombers to get in their licks. The landing craft roared toward the lagoon under the cover of massive fire.

Then things went wrong:

1. Five hundred yards from shore—five football fields away—the landing craft hit a submerged reef that they could not get over.
2. At the same time that this unexpected obstacle interfered with the naval commander's plan, the island's Japanese defenders let loose with their entire arsenal of weapons.
3. The Marines, being Marines, jumped over the sides of their stranded craft and began to wade ashore. Few in the first wave made it.

Envision what that was like: No planned alternatives. No cover. No concealment. Advancing with heavy loads through water that in some places was over their heads. For over five hundred yards. A running back who gains a hundred yards in a football game is considered to have done something tremendous—but no one's shooting at him, and he isn't in water up to his neck and carrying over a hundred pounds of gear. These men were the definition of heroes.

4. The naval bombardment had caused few casualties among the Japanese, who had taken shelter in bunkers and then rushed out to their positions during the brief lull between the end of the shelling and the landing.

5. It took the Marines four successive waves—with the three follow-on waves still coming despite the fact that they had seen what had happened to those before them—before they were able to establish a tentative toehold on the island: they controlled twenty feet inland up to the seawall, and a beachhead one hundred yards wide. Less than the size of a football field.

The cost in blood for the naval admiral's poor understanding of the environment surrounding Tarawa was high. Out of five thousand men in the first four waves, over fifteen hundred were dead or wounded.

But the Marines kept coming and by sheer weight of numbers, and outstanding courage, they began to expand the beachhead. In the seventy-six hours it took to conquer the tiny atoll of Tarawa, over one thousand Americans died and twenty-three hundred were wounded.

The lesson

Tarawa was costly in blood, but in the long run it saved lives as the Navy and Marines realized they had to change what they were doing. The Higgins boats that had been used as landing craft were removed from that task, and amtracs, capable of crawling over reefs such as the one at Tarawa, replaced them.

More important, the UDTs—Underwater Demolition Teams—

the forerunners of the Navy SEALs, were formed to find and destroy natural and man-made obstacles before landings took place. They were formed to conduct area studies.

SPECIAL FORCES AREA STUDY

In Special Forces the first thing we did in mission planning after being given our *What* (goal) and our *Why* (intent) was to conduct a detailed area study. An area study is a thorough examination of an operating environment. We wanted to see what elements in the environment would affect us, and, as important, what effect we would have on the environment.

Ultimately, an area study is the same thing as research.

In isolation (locked up in a secure compound 24/7 to do mission planning) we'd bring in area experts (CIA agents, State Department personnel, people who'd traveled there, locals, academics, etc.) to tell us about the environment we were heading into. It pays to listen to people who are currently at or have been where you want your path to take you.

The purpose of a Special Forces area study is to outline details about the area being studied.

For a Special Forces area study, the following are critical factors:

- Civil populace
- Military and paramilitary forces
- Economic factors
- Political characteristics
- Resistance forces

- Geography, hydrography, climate
- Potential targets
- Culture, norms, taboos

In the next exercise, you'll do a rudimentary area study of your environment. You can do separate ones for your home life, your work environment, your social environment, etc. But in the end, you need to pull them all together into one complete study of your total environment.

While the Special Operations Forces area study is specific to conducting military operations, you can see how you can use this template in your own life. Pretty much everything you need for your own path to success has been done by someone else. Yes, you do have to make it specific to your life, but why not use as much of what others have already learned to your advantage? Just as it's important in Special Forces training to study history, you need to study the history that is applicable to your life.

Study those who have succeeded and failed. For example, if you want to be a successful scientist, you have to study other scientists, both current and past. How did they achieve what they did? What failures did they encounter on the way, and how did they deal with them?

Overnight successes are few and far between. Among many aspiring writers, I sometimes find an attitude that glittering success can be theirs with just one book. One masterpiece. Yes, that happens once in a while, but it is rare. Most successful writers spend many years and many books working their way up. They learn the craft and then become artists.

Studying and research can help shorten the learning curve of your path and help you avoid the pitfalls that inexperience inevitably brings. This is the reason I am very big on SOPs (Standing Operating Procedures, covered in Tool Seven).

And don't forget the effect of environment on you. Can you achieve what you want to, given the situation in which you are living?

Consult subject matter experts to get their knowledge and expertise. Study how other people have achieved either exactly what you want to achieve, or goals similar to yours. While you may believe your goal is unique, the odds are that others have blazed the same or similar paths before you. Learn from their experiences. Your personal area study may actually show you that you can't achieve your successful goal in your environment and thus you have to change your environment.

Jack Canfield, the co-creator of the *Chicken Soup* books, advises people who want to succeed to get away from toxic people. Sometimes you also need to get away from toxic places.

Your area study of your personal and work environment will identify potential sources of conflict and positive support. Your personal area study helps you define the environment in which you live, the environment's effect on you, and your effect on it.

Exercise 6: WHERE

Take a piece of paper. Fold it in thirds. In the left column write down the *What* you listed in column one of Exercise 4.

Label the middle column *My WHERE As It Is Now.*

Label the right column *My WHERE As It Should Be.*

List in the middle column those people and things that currently are part of your *Where* and how they affect it.

List in the right column how you would like your *Where* to be in order for it to be a positive environment.

Note where there is a large gap between the listings in the two columns. The difference between your *As Is* and your *Should Be* shows you where you need to effect change in your environment. It shows you the gap in your life between where you are now and where you would like to be. These are changes that this book will help you make.

Exercise 7: WHERE

Using the four-column sheet from Exercise 4, fill out the third column. Next to each *What* and *Why*, list the *Where* as it should be in the third column.

Hopefully, you can see how *Who Dares Wins* exercises will help you break up your goals into manageable pieces. Imagine how much more you'll know about what you want and how to make that happen once you've completed the exercises in all nine tools.

WHERE: THE ARTIST'S IMAGINATION

When I write, part of my area study is the *research* I do for a book: studying the setting for the book, the characters, the point of view I'm going to write in, the narrative structure, and so on.

After my students nail down their *What* and *Why*, one thing I recommend they do is what I call a book dissection. I have them read a book similar to the one they want to write and analyze it—not so they can plagiarize the work, but so they can see how someone else successfully wrote a similar book.

It's always wise to learn from the masters.

I don't restrict the *Where* to the book. I also tell the students to do an area study of the business environment in which they plan to work: the roles of agents and editors, the publishing business, trends, readers—in sum, the entertainment business.

WINS, THE GREEN BERET WAY

Let's pull together *What, Why,* and *Where.*

Let me give you two examples, one at a very high level that didn't have positive alignment among the three tools and one at the Special Forces level that did.

NEGATIVE ALIGNMENT EXAMPLE—1941, JAPAN VERSUS THE UNITED STATES

What: The Japanese fleet will destroy the American fleet and change the balance of power in the Pacific.

Why: The stated *Why* to Admiral Yamamoto, who commanded the Japanese fleet, was to negate American sea power in the Pacific so the Japanese could conduct other operations. This *Why* was attainable. However, there were some high up in the Japanese government who believed the real reason *Why* they were doing the *What*—destroying the fleet—was to force the United States to sue for peace and retreat from the Pacific theater. This is where alignment started to unravel. Yamamoto, who had traveled extensively in the States, thought this intent was not attainable. He feared, rightly, that the attack would "awaken a sleeping giant." Thus, if his analysis of the hidden *Why* had been heeded, the *What* would have had to be changed or dropped.

Where: Pearl Harbor. Delving deeper, the Japanese did not do an effective area study of their *Where* to support their *What*

45

and *Why*. Even though they were using aircraft carriers to conduct the attack, they did not make certain the American aircraft carriers were present in the harbor on the day of the attack. Instead, they focused on the battleships. The very success of their own attack would prove that battleships were obsolete—an inherent paradox the planners did not consider. Also, they could have greatly negated even the absent carriers' ability to carry on operations if they had focused on destroying the port infrastructure rather than just the ships, particularly by attacking the massive fuel reserves in the area. Remember when we discussed that *Why* allows you to innovate? Negating the American fleet could have been done in ways other than trying to directly destroy the fleet, if the planners had been more innovative in using the *Why*.

The Japanese had a spectacular apparent success attacking Pearl Harbor, but there was a subordinate goal under the primary one that they failed to achieve: wiping out the American aircraft carriers, which were at sea during the attack. So both *Why*'s weren't achieved: they did not negate American sea power in the Pacific, because the air power associated with it was intact along with the support infrastructure, especially the fuel supply. As Yamamoto had feared, the Americans did not sue for peace. They declared war.

A more careful study of *Where* might have avoided failure on both *Why*'s and changed the *What*. First, by listening to experts on Americans, such as Yamamoto, the Japanese high command would have realized the Americans would fight instead of surrender. Second, by doing an area study of the target just before the attack, they would have learned the aircraft carriers were not present and perhaps could have come up with an alternate plan to complete that important part of the goal. They also might have targeted the fuel depots and crippled the fleet indirectly for an extensive period of time. They also might have picked specific targets to sink in the shipping channels of the harbor to deny ingress and egress for an extended period of time.

Do you see how important it is to integrate *What, Why,* and *Where?*

What the Japanese failed to use is a tool that integrates *What, Why,* and *Where:* the Special Forces CARVER formula. Let me describe CARVER to you, then show you an example where it was successfully used.

THE CARVER FORMULA

CARVER is a formula we use in Special Forces to assess targets for specific missions. It is the way we integrate *What, Why,* and *Where* and come up with the best possible solution for success.

When a Special Forces soldier gets a mission, he is given the *What* (goal/target) and *Why* (intent) and a *Where* (target and area of operations). He is not told *how* the job is to be done.

The CARVER formula is then applied to assess the target in the following terms:

CRITICALITY: How important is the target? What are the critical nodes of the target? For example, to put a port out of commission for a while, a critical node might be the shipping channel. Or the cranes that load and off-load cargo. Or Pearl Harbor's fuel depot.

ACCESSIBILITY: Can the target be gotten to? How? Can the part of the target that is to be destroyed be accessed? There are often many critical nodes, but some are more easily attacked than others.

RECOGNIZABILITY: Can the target be recognized? Can the critical nodes be located?

VULNERABILITY: Will the team have the capability to actually destroy the target? For example, a dam requires a tremendous amount of force to breach, normally more explosives than a team could carry in. But to overcome this limitation, a team could use a laser designator to guide bombs or cruise missiles in to a target. Never accept limitations at first—there are usually ways to overcome them.

EFFECT: What effect, outside of damage to the target itself, will destroying the target have? For example, a team might have the mission to destroy a bridge that the enemy uses to carry supplies over. But will destroying that bridge have too great a negative effect on the population?

RECUPERABILITY: How long will it take to fix the damage done to the target?

CARVER is a way intent can be assessed, tunnel vision can be avoided, and a *What* can be achieved, satisfying the *Why* under the constraints and opportunities of *Where*.

POSITIVE ALIGNMENT EXAMPLE—THE A-TEAM

My team was assigned a mission to destroy a strategic oil pipeline. We were given the parameters of making the pipeline nonoperational for a minimum of seven days.

What: We will destroy the pipeline.

Why: To deny the enemy oil from it for seven days.

Where: We were given the entire length of the pipeline from which to pick the specific point we wanted to attack in order to achieve our *What* and *Why*.

The problem

We learned that destroying a normal section of the pipe would achieve the *What* (destroy the pipeline) but not achieve the *Why*: the repair estimate for a damaged section was forty-eight hours. Just walking up to the pipe and blowing it was out.

The solution

The demolitions men began searching for *critical nodes* by doing an area study (*Where*). The thing about critical nodes in targets, though, is that the people who own the target also usually recognize these spots and put extra protection on them. We knew destroying a pump station would achieve the *Why*, but the pump stations were well guarded. The odds of successfully destroying one with the assets we had on the team were limited.

We looked at the pipeline terminus to see if we could destroy the means by which the oil was transferred out of the pipeline and onto further conveyances. However, we were not allowed to attack the port because the effect would have been greater than the simple loss of the pipeline. Even though an attack that resulted in blocking the channel to oil tankers would have achieved the *What* and *Why*, we couldn't do it. It would also have resulted in undesirable effects, including severe environmental damage.

We kept looking, going along the hundreds of miles of pipeline imagery. Then we found it. The pipeline crossed rivers in two places. Over one of those rivers the pipeline was held up by a suspension bridge consisting of two towers and cables. We consulted with experts (area study research) and learned that if we blew the cables, the weight of the oil in the length of pipe suspended over the river would be too much to sustain and that section would rip free.

The repair timeline on the pipe over the river was different than that for the pipe on the ground, as a barge with a crane would have to be brought upriver. Estimates ranged from one week to two.

Security at the crossing was a barbed wire fence and video surveillance, both of which we could overcome. Apparently the enemy did not realize the significance of this site and had no security force guarding it.

The result

We did have to consider the ecological effect of the oil that would be let loose into the river, but the nearest pump station was only a few miles away and as soon as pressure was lost on the pipe, the pump station would shut down.

We had our critical node that satisfied CARVER. We could achieve the assigned goal.

CARVER AND YOUR GOALS

Sometimes CARVER led my Special Forces team to change a mission goal. When you start researching your environment (in your area study) and examining your intent, don't be disturbed if you end up adjusting your goals as well.

CARVER is not a step-by-step process, but rather an interactive overview. The questions in CARVER can be answered in any order. You'll develop all the answers you need as you work through the *Who Dares Wins* nine tools within your Circle of Success.

To expand your personal area study, ask yourself these CARVER questions:

CRITICALITY:
- How important is my goal?
- What are the critical parts (nodes) of my goal?
- What is the key to achieving this goal?
- How many other people can do what I want to achieve?

ACCESSIBILITY:
- Can the goal be achieved?
- Can it be achieved with my available resources?
- How can I get to the goal from where I am now?
- If this access point is a critical node, can I actually reach it?

RECOGNIZABILITY:
- Can I clearly see my goal and state it?
- Do I clearly know *why* I want to achieve this goal?
- How might I be sidetracked in achieving my goal?
- Will the process of achieving my goal overwhelm the end result?

VULNERABILITY:
- Am I capable of achieving my goal?
- If I don't have the capability, what help is needed?

- Do I have the resources to achieve my goal?
- If I don't have the resources, what help is needed?

EFFECT:

- What effect will achieving my goal have on me?
- What effect will achieving my goal have on those around me?
- What effect will achieving my goal have on my environment?

RECUPERABILITY:

- Will my effort achieve the desired results?
- What are the possible undesired results?
- Can I sustain my effort, or will I revert to old habits?

Exercise 8: WINS

Using your four-column sheet from Exercise 4, pick one of the *What*'s. Using the *Why* and *Where* you've already added, apply the CARVER formula to the goal to see if you can achieve it. If you can, then you can check column four—*Done*.

This doesn't mean the *What* is actually done; it means your planning for it is done. You can apply this formula to all your *What*'s.

Now that you have an idea of **What** your goals are, **Why** you want to achieve your goals, and how to refine your **What** and **Why** based on **Where** you will be operating, it's time to move to Area Two: WHO.

WHO

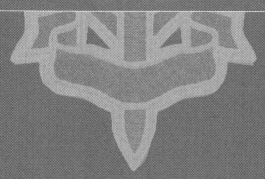

You must understand your character.

You must understand what true change is, factor in fear,
and use courage to move beyond the fear.

"Therefore I say: Know the enemy and know yourself; in a hundred battles you will never be in peril."

—SUN TZU

In Area Two, you'll create a plan for change. Use the tools in this section to look deep into yourself and discover what you want to change, so you can achieve your Area One goals.

We'll start with *Character* so you understand yourself and others. Then learn what true *Change* is and how to accomplish it. And finally learn how you can utilize *Courage* to conquer fear and be the person you want to be.

Character is the essence of a person. Your character is made up of both your strengths and your weaknesses. It's important to understand yourself, especially your blind spot, before taking action to achieve your goals. Your blind spot is wrapped around your deepest fears. A successful individual doesn't ignore fear, but rather faces it, plans for it, and factors it into his or her life with courage. If you want to succeed the Green Beret way, facing and planning for fear is essential.

MOST OF WHAT YOU DO IS HABIT

"Not choice, but habit rules the unreflecting herd."

—WILLIAM WORDSWORTH

The tools in *Who Dares Wins* help you consciously change your habits, and through the Circle of Success, your life. You have to train yourself to question your repeated behaviors.

I'm not talking about a radical change that will occur instantaneously. This book teaches you incremental, day-by-day change— what the Japanese call *kaizen* (continual improvement). Small changes, added together, day after day, lead to new habits and a new life. Your focus will be not only on the end result, but on the continuous process. When you finish Tool Nine, you won't be done, but you will be changed.

I focus a great deal on fear for someone who is teaching about success, because changing habits is not for the faint of heart. Most of us like comfort and security. Change brings about discomfort and fear.

A little change brings discomfort. A lot of change brings fear. There is a very thin line between discomfort and fear. The more you are willing to face and conquer your fears, the further out you push that line and the more change you'll bring about as you venture further into your Courage Zone, which increases your Comfort Zone. In fact, as you'll learn, there are benefits to fear.

TOOL FOUR

UNDERSTAND YOUR *CHARACTER*

INTRODUCTION

"Invincibility depends on one's self; the enemy's vulnerability on him."

—SUN TZU

You need to understand your own character as it is now, before you set off to change. It helps to know who you are when you're starting, before you can successfully navigate your path to where you're going and who you want to be. Being aware of your flaws and blind spots is key. These can trip you up when you start pursuing your life goals.

Not understanding your complete character can lead to goals and a path generated by fear—a recipe for failure, not success.

SPECIAL FORCES ASSESSMENT AND SELECTION THOUGHT:

The only person holding you back is you; everyone else is merely watching.

BLOOD LESSON: NEVER GIVE UP

Let's look at *Character* profiles for two legendary Special Forces officers.

The problem

Nick Rowe: 1960: graduated from West Point. 1963: went to Vietnam with the Special Forces, at a time when most Americans couldn't tell you where Vietnam was. October 29, 1963: on patrol with Captain "Rocky" Versace and Sergeant Daniel Pitzer, advising a Civilian Irregular Defense Group company, searching for a small enemy unit reportedly in the area.

Captain Versace: on his second tour in Vietnam, after volunteering to stay to help the people he loved; planned to enter a seminary upon his return; only two weeks away from coming back to the States when he volunteered for the October 29 patrol.

At ten in the morning, the patrol's pursuit of the enemy triggered an ambush. After fighting until late afternoon, the unit was overrun and the two officers were captured. The Viet Cong's focus was to break American captives' will, so they could extract tactical information.

Two solutions

Captain "Rocky" Versace

"Captain Humbert R. Versace distinguished himself by extraordinary heroism during the period of 29 October 1963 to 26 September 1965, while serving as S-2 Advisor, Military Assistance Advisory Group, Detachment 52, Ca Mau, Republic of Vietnam. While accompanying a Civilian Irregular Defense Group patrol engaged in combat operations in Thoi Binh District, An Xuyen Province, Captain Versace and the patrol came under sudden and intense mortar, automatic weapons, and small arms fire from elements of a heavily armed enemy battalion.

"As the battle raged, Captain Versace, although severely wounded

in the knee and back by hostile fire, fought valiantly and continued to engage enemy targets. Weakened by his wounds and fatigued by the fierce firefight, Captain Versace stubbornly resisted capture by the over-powering Viet Cong force with the last full measure of his strength and ammunition. Taken prisoner by the Viet Cong, he exemplified the tenets of the Code of Conduct from the time he entered into Prisoner of War status. Captain Versace assumed command of his fellow American soldiers, scorned the enemy's exhaustive interrogation and indoctrination efforts, and made three unsuccessful attempts to escape, despite his weakened condition, which was brought about by his wounds and the extreme privation and hardships he was forced to endure.

"During his captivity, Captain Versace was segregated in an isolated prisoner of war cage, manacled in irons for prolonged periods of time, and placed on extremely reduced ration. The enemy was unable to break his indomitable will, his faith in God, and his trust in the United States of America. Captain Versace, an American fighting man who epitomized the principles of his country and the Code of Conduct, was executed by the Viet Cong on 26 September 1965. Captain Versace's gallant actions in close contact with an enemy force and unyielding courage and bravery while a prisoner of war are in the highest traditions of the military service and reflect the utmost credit upon himself and the United States Army."

—from the Medal of Honor citation

Captain Versace exemplified the true spirit of the Special Forces soldier, both in combat and in captivity. In both situations, he remained consistent and true to his character. When he was isolated from the other prisoners, they knew he was still there because he would sing "God Bless America" at the top of his lungs.

In his first attempt to escape, because of wounds to his legs, he crawled.

Nick Rowe

Nick Rowe spent sixty-two months in captivity. Every day he could expect to face the same fate as his friend. He suffered from dysentery, beriberi, fungal diseases, malnutrition, and torture. He lived in a wooden cage three feet by four by six.

When interrogated, Rowe deceived the Viet Cong about his background. He told them he was a draftee and an engineer and his job was to build schools. He said he had gone to a small liberal college. To test him, the Viet Cong gave him engineering problems to solve. Because West Point had numerous mandatory engineering courses, Rowe passed these tests. Rowe's cover story was eventually blown through no fault of his own.

An American antiwar activist group came to North Vietnam. They asked to speak to POWs to see if they were being treated fairly. On the top of their list was Rowe's name, along with his real background and assignment. Note that this group had failed to do an effective area study of where they were going and the effect of their actions went beyond the immediate result they desired—with almost tragic results.

Rowe was taken out into a swamp and staked down naked for two days. He still refused to talk, even though the information he knew was now dated and useless. He later escaped with another wounded POW. Chased and about to be caught, the other POW urged Rowe to go on. He did so, but stopped when he heard the Viet Cong calling out that they would execute the other man if he did not come back. So he came back.

Would you have done the same?

In December 1968, over five years after he'd been captured, Rowe was taken out to be executed. The Viet Cong had had enough, and they knew any information he had was worthless.

As they took him to the place of his death, several American helicopters flew overhead. Rowe took advantage of the diversion, striking down his guards and running into a clearing. Despite being malnourished and dressed in black pajamas, he was recognized as a westerner. A helicopter swooped down and picked him up.

In 1971 he published his story, *Five Years to Freedom*, and re-tired from active duty to write full-time. But in 1981, his country reached out to him. Because of his unique expertise, he was brought to the JFK Special Warfare Center and School at Fort Bragg to design a training course called SERE: Survival, Evasion, Resistance, and Escape. The course is still in existence today and has helped thousands of American soldiers.

The lesson

Versace and Rowe are classic examples of men who exerted strong personal *Character* under adverse conditions. Yes, these were extreme examples, but in your life you will in various ways face extreme tests to your character. Both Versace and Rowe became men who exhibited such courage not only because of innate abilities, but also because of the training they received as Green Berets.

No matter what pressure was brought on them, what their level of fear was, they stayed true to what they believed in. Equally important: they remained true to their comrades.

WHAT IS CHARACTER?

Character is the combination of qualities or features that distinguishes one person from another. *Character* is the key to *Who Dares Wins:* looking at the world around you differently from others and understanding yourself. Having the self-confidence that comes with an integrated character that you clearly understand, both good and bad, is key.

Too many people are locked into a limited worldview because their own character keeps them from seeing the true nature of the world around them. Your view of others and the world around you is colored by your point of view. If you understand your point of view, you'll have a more realistic view of yourself and others.

Exercise 9: CHARACTER

Define yourself in one sentence.

Which of the following areas did you use in your definition?

- Work
- Position
- Family
- Background
- Schooling
- Education level
- Marital status
- Sexual orientation
- Age
- Race

Do you define others by the same, or different, terms? You are now getting an idea of your point of view. Remember, everyone doesn't share your point of view. Understanding your point of view shapes the way you view others and makes your reality different from their reality. The best reality to be in is the one based on action.

STUDY YOUR ACTIONS TO UNDERSTAND YOUR CHARACTER

In Special Forces, we learned that a person tends to show his true nature by his actions/reactions during a crisis. You learn a lot about people by observing what choices they make under pressure.

Actions speak louder than words.

Actions are a *What*. As we learned in Area One, you should also try to figure out the corresponding *Why* for each *What*. The same *What* done for two different *Why*'s (intent) makes the actions very different.

Not only must you observe an action and the intent, you must have an understanding of the environment the action is taken in (*Where*) to help you interpret motivation (*Why*).

In schools such as Special Forces Assessment and Selection, Ranger School, Scuba School, Airborne School, etc., this basic tenet of acting under constant stress and crisis is drilled into students while they are performing under extreme pressure. Incoming plebes' first summer at West Point is called Beast Barracks, which gives you an idea of the environment they face.

The harshness of this kind of training is often explained by saying the instructors must first "break a person down" before they can rebuild him. I believe this method strips away any façade a person has and drills down to his true nature.

UNDERSTAND YOUR TRUE NATURE

Those whose true nature cannot handle a specific situation will either quit or fail. People who do not succeed in Beast Barracks, Ranger School, SEAL training, and Special Forces Assessment and Selection, etc., are not bad people or failures. They just do not belong in the environments those training programs are designed to prepare them for. In the same way, you have to understand your true nature so you can choose a path of change you are capable of completing. Keep in mind that this harsh phase of breaking someone down is a form of making the person surrender. The more the person fights the change, the harsher the resulting process. To change, you have to surrender to the fact that who you are now and what you're doing isn't working, and that the more you fight yourself, the more that fight will be projected into your world with harsh, negative effects.

Exercise 10: CHARACTER

On the same sheet you used for Exercise 9, describe a moment when you were under extreme stress and pressure and had to make a decision. List the cause of the stress and pressure.

Exercise 11: CHARACTER

On the same sheet you used for Exercises 9 and 10, describe your reaction to that moment and the decision you made.

In retrospect, was it a good decision, or could you have chosen better?

YOUR PRIMARY MOTIVATOR

People who are successful have a readily identifiable primary motivator that allows them to overcome great obstacles and succeed. People who have a meaning in their life can transcend suffering and find success. They can live well in the face of fear.

Some people might already have found their meaning of life. Others may need to find one. In Special Forces training, the candidates are forced to perform under extreme duress. They not only accept challenges but conquer them. They're forced to dig deep, to find what really motivates them. The desire just to wear a Green Beret and call themselves Special Forces doesn't work. Those candidates who want the superficial aspects because of the way others will view them fall to the wayside. In the same way, I've noticed many people want what they think the lifestyle of an author is, but they don't have the wherewithal to *be* an author.

In Exercise 2, you were asked to write down what motivates you the most. Look back at your answer. Is it truly your primary motivator?

SUCCESSFUL CHARACTER TRAITS

Special Forces Assessment and Selection is based on successful character traits. Studying some of these will help you understand your true nature.

Open-mindedness

How willing are you to change? Are you willing to learn from any source that helps you improve yourself? If you are not where you want to be, then you must change something, rather than waiting for the world to come to you.

Because, guess what?

It isn't.

So how do you use being open-minded to change? You need a . . .

Willingness to surrender when wrong

To change, you have to be willing to say the three hardest words for many people: "I am wrong." Followed by, "Maybe I'm not doing this the best possible way. Maybe I can learn to do this better." You must be willing to surrender. You must be willing to change based on the feedback you receive from the exercises in this book.

A Stanford psychologist, Carol Dweck, found something interesting when studying talented people and how they performed. She discovered that those people who believe they were born with all the talent and intelligence they need approach the world with a "fixed" mind-set. They rarely change. Why should they?

Those who believe that they weren't born with everything they need, and believe they can expand their abilities and become better, approach the world with a "growth" mind-set. Guess which of the two are more successful? The latter reach their creative potential, while the former rarely live up to their potential. In Special Forces, volunteering for the training and successfully completing it indicates a willingness to grow. I found the same to be true of writers: I often saw extremely talented writers fail, while those with lesser talent but greater open-mindedness and perseverance succeeded.

There are so few highly successful people and organizations, because few people and organizations are willing to learn and change. Change is also difficult because it requires not just change in your actions but also . . .

Emotional change

Once you've accepted the need for change and surrendered your current position and mental outlook, you've intellectually accepted the change. You then change your actions, which we will discuss in more detail later in this book. As you change, it affects you emotionally over time.

Emotional change can take years but you have to stick with it.

Change usually requires Elizabeth Kübler-Ross's five emotional stages.

1. DENIAL: "There is no problem or need to change."
2. ANGER: "How dare someone, including me, say I'm not doing it right."
3. BARGAINING: "Maybe if I can change some small things, it will make a big difference."
4. DEPRESSION: "There's too much to change. I'm overwhelmed."
5. ACCEPTANCE: "I will do it."

Which does lead to real change.

Note that these are Kübler-Ross's stages of death and dying! To change you have to "kill off" your old self.

Exercise 12: CHARACTER

Describe the last time you were told you were doing something wrong and how you responded to it.

  Describe your reaction in terms of the five parts of the Kübler-Ross scale.

  Did you make it to acceptance and change?

  If not, where did you stop and why?

If you didn't make it all the way to acceptance, don't worry. This book will help you get there and change. Remember, that's Tool Five, coming next.

Two things that can motivate you to try to change and also stick with it are two apparently paradoxical emotions . . .

Desire and contentment

Desire is the stick that drives the successful to achieve more. The carrot. What do you desire? What do you want?

Note I say want, not need. There is a big difference between a need and a want. A need is something that you don't have control over desiring. A want is something you can control.

A successful individual must climb above his needs and focus on his wants.

Contentment is the reward for achieving your desires. You can't constantly be in a state of desire all the time. At least occasionally, you must get to that point of achievement, or frustration will rule. For a person to enjoy life, there must be a degree of contentment in the here and now. What is the point of being successful if you can't enjoy it? Every once in a while you need to focus on what has been achieved.

A successful person needs to balance desire and contentment.

Exercise 13: CHARACTER

Take a piece of paper. Draw a line down the middle. Label the left side *To Do*. Label the right side *Done*.

List down the left side everything you have to do tomorrow.

Then, when you do one of your *To Do*'s, cross it off *and* write what you've done on the right side. Thus you can literally see your balance between desire and contentment on one page for one day.

Use this technique on a daily basis to give yourself positive feedback. Crossing something off a list isn't quite as satisfying emotionally as listing something achieved.

As part of desire and contentment, you must also be able to "close doors." We waste time pursuing too many options. One of the purposes of Area One of this book was to help you lock down your *What*, your goals. Discarding goals that aren't what you really want can help you focus on those you do.

The French philosopher Jean Buridan tells this parable known as "Buridan's Ass": A hungry donkey enters a barnyard. There are equal-sized bales of hay to either side. The donkey remains frozen, unable to choose one, afraid that by doing so, it will not get the other. Eventually the donkey starves to death.

Ever felt like that donkey?

Closing doors can give you great focus. When we have too many options, we don't focus on the ones we should.

Exercise 14: CHARACTER

Look at your *To Do/Done* list from Exercise 13. Are there some *To Do*'s that aren't really needed, that you've actually had on your *To Do* list a long time and never gotten around to? Maybe you shouldn't do them at all. Close some doors. Get rid of options that distract from your main goals. Are there people in your life you hold on to and expend energy on out of fear?

Patience and self-discipline

Too many people rely on the outside world to enforce patience and supply discipline. A successful person internalizes both traits. The Special Forces Qualification Course takes roughly a year— interestingly, the average time many authors spend on a book. Neither task is a recipe for instant gratification. Taking a year to achieve a goal is something that requires a great deal of patience and discipline.

When I taught martial arts, the majority of the new students quit shortly after the first month. Students came in and wanted to become Bruce Lee rolled into Jackie Chan, all within a couple of weeks. When they realized it would take years of boring, repetitive, very hard work, the majority gave up. It doesn't take any special skill up front to become a black belt—just a lot of time and effort to develop special skills. The same is true of pretty much anything you want to achieve.

If you are patient enough to do the long-term work, you will pull ahead of the pack and become successful. To do so, you must have a long-term perspective of your major goals.

To keep focused during long-term work, you must accept that the payoff usually comes later rather than sooner. Delayed gratification is one of the keys to self-discipline. Self-discipline is one of the keys to developing self-confidence.

One way to make a long-term goal achievable and not overwhelming is to break it down into subordinate goals that are closer and more easily achievable. For example, in the Special Forces Qualification Course there are numerous phases. As the candidates pass each phase, they feel a sense of accomplishment that encourages them to finish the entire course. Also, if candidates have a problem in a particular phase, they always have the option to redo just that phase, rather than the entire course. As a writer, I can break a book down to a number of pages to write per day or a number of chapters per month. I can write a scene, just to get the bones of it down, and then come back to it, improving the writing.

An active imagination

In many ways life is like a chess game: to be successful, you have to think a half dozen moves ahead, while considering the impact of your opponent's decisions (and in life, your environment). This means choosing a successful strategic direction among a very large number of variables. And as you've just learned, your plans must take into account your personality.

Make your creative plans based on acting within your character—much like chess strategy is dependent on a piece being capable of a specific type of move—and then, once you've mastered that, press the limits of your character to expand your capabilities, venturing into your Courage Zone. You'll get an idea of your character template shortly and how to expand what I call your Comfort Zone (Tool Six) so that you are capable of more and more moves.

Set your imagination free to plot numerous paths. From these, based on all the variables facing you, you can choose the one that stands out above the others—the successful or critical path.

As in chess, a successful person in life must be able to see a problem in its entirety, and then be able to break a solution down into manageable steps (moves). You must be able to see beyond the current move, to each move's implications.

Don't get tunnel vision. For example, a visiting professor from the Colorado School of Mines teaching at West Point once presented his students with a problem to test their imaginations:

A two-foot metal pipe is welded vertically to a steel plate. It is just barely wide enough to slide a ping-pong ball into. The students' job was to get the ball out of the pipe without damaging the ball. The only tools given the students were a pair of pliers, a coat hanger, a magnet, and a comb.

The professor let the class war-game this problem for a while, then listened to various proposals, none of which worked. His solution used none of the tools listed—he'd given them as distracters. To get the ball out, simply urinate into the pipe until the ball floated out. But because we'd been given those tools, every solution focused on using those items rather than on the problem.

The ability to set goals

In Area One: Wins, you learned the importance of specifying your goals, understanding why you want to achieve them, and studying the situation in which you want to become successful.

One thing you can do without is procrastination. *Procrastination* comes from two Latin words:

Pro: For. *Cras:* Tomorrow.

Not only must you set your goals (*What*), you must also set deadlines for your goals. People with firm deadlines written down get better results than those without.

Exercise 15: CHARACTER

Remember the four-column *What, Why, Where, Done* list you began in Exercise 4? For every *What* that has not been *Done*, pencil in a deadline for when it should be done.

The clock is now ticking.

Emotion and intellect

As an author I work in the entertainment business, which is an oxymoron. Entertainment runs on emotion, while business runs on logic (supposedly). But no matter what business you're in, emotion is a significant factor that can't be quantified.

Why is a certain book a bestseller and another not? Why does one movie break box office records and another doesn't? If the answers to these questions could be put into a formula, then everyone would be following the formula and every book would be a bestseller, every movie a blockbuster.

Why do we do things that ultimately hurt ourselves? In lucid moments we know they make no sense. But then we go out and do them anyway. In these situations, emotion is overwhelming your logic.

Many individuals and organizations don't value the power of emotion.

It is important to realize there are two sets of norms in your life: social norms and market norms. Understand clearly the line between the two. Your personal relationships belong in the realm of social norms. Social norms are based on emotion. Your business relationships are usually in the realm of market norms. Market norms are based on money.

When a market norm collides with a social norm, the social norm is the loser and is easily lost and very hard to recover. For example, if you offered your spouse money for picking you up at the airport, you would be bringing a market norm into the social realm and your spouse would most likely be offended.

Conversely, social norms are more powerful than market norms in terms of motivation. This comes into play in *Who Dares Wins* because, interestingly enough, Special Forces operates more on social norms than market norms. Jobs where one is asked to put his or her life on the line can't function well under market norms—how much can you pay someone for their life? Thus police, firefighters, and military tend to operate under social norms, where pride in one's profession, teamwork and care for comrades, and a sense of duty are more important than money.

Professional athletes present a curious case because coaches face the difficult job of trying to merge social norms (for motivation and team-building) with market norms (because it is a business). There is a trend nowadays in which businesses try to bring social norms into the workplace. While this can be very effective, it can also be very dangerous, if there is no consistency in the application of the social norms in the work environment.

In your life, recognize that the way you interact with other people emotionally—social norms—is much more important than any market norms interaction.

Anger and guilt

Two emotional blind spots for many people are anger and guilt. These emotions are often indicators of a weakness you need to deal with. And until you do, that weakness can keep you from exploring your full potential and can derail you from achieving your goals.

Whenever you experience anger or guilt, focus on what is going on. Figure out when the emotion is appropriate, and understand when it isn't.

Anger and guilt are often brought about by things that normally shouldn't trigger it: frequently, these emotions are responses that became a habit in childhood. While both are necessary at times, many people are so consumed by anger and guilt that these negative emotions become a shackle around their lives.

When a person gets angry about something someone else is doing, it is often a sign of a flaw in the angry person's character. When a person feels guilty about something happening in their life, it is often an inappropriate response to reality. We use these two facts in Special Forces training to build a person's character.

Flash points

During prisoner of war (SERE—survival, evasion, resistance, and escape) training (developed by Colonel Rowe) run by Special Forces, one thing the instructors do to participants is try to find their flash points—things that make a prisoner react angrily or with guilt.

If captors can find a prisoner's flash point and exploit it, they can delve deeper and find the prisoner's greatest fears. This allows the captors to break the prisoner much more quickly. Left unchallenged, your mind can become its own kind of prison, where your flash points and greatest fears will work against you with increasing frequency.

The key to the training is that once the candidates go through this experience and are aware of their flash points, they can strengthen themselves in those areas and are less likely to react to a flash point in the future and in a real SERE situation.

Anger and guilt spring out of fear, usually on a subconscious level. You'll learn later that working through your mind's defense barriers is the second step of emotional change. As you become more conscious of your blind spots and flaws, you gain more control over them.

Exercise 16: CHARACTER

Describe the last time you felt anger or guilt. (If you can't remember, then notice the *next* time you feel either of those emotions.) Write the event down. What specifically provoked the emotion? Why did this situation touch your flash point? Simply understanding this dynamic will make you stronger the next time your flash point is touched.

CHARACTER TEMPLATES

Successful individuals adopt a psychological structure for character types—so they can better understand their own character and others'. Fortunately, structures already exist and have been thoroughly developed by behavior and motivation experts. I recommend studying various templates and recommend two here:

Profiling

Character type profiling is regularly used by Special Forces and law enforcement, a fact that has been repeatedly fictionalized in pop culture: books, movies, and television. A profiler examines the results of an action and works backward, trying to come up with the character type that would perform such an act.

When Special Forces was founded, a list of character traits for the type of person needed to operate in this elite unit was drawn up, based on experiences in guerrilla warfare and covert operations in World War II. Then they went and looked for those types of people.

A key to profiling is that people have character traits that dictate their actions. This is understandable because most of what we do is habit. Also, the brain doesn't start from scratch in every situation—we have imprinted stereotypes that shape our actions. We consciously control very little of our day-to-day life and decision-making.

Members of the Behavioral Science Unit of the FBI began their study of profiling by going to prisons and interviewing every living serial killer, to see what type of person was capable of doing such horrible acts. Patterns were identified in the killers' backgrounds, their thought processes, the way they conducted their crimes, and so on. In the same manner, you can study patterns in your and others' daily lives.

You can determine which of your life patterns are positive, and which are negative, then work on getting rid of the negative ones and replacing them with positive ones.

By profiling yourself, you can make more conscious choices, rather than react emotionally and out of blind habit.

Exercise 17: CHARACTER

For the next twenty-four hours, write down everything you do. Simply list every action without comment. Let the list sit for several days. Then look at the list with an open mind. Describe what kind of person would do these things.

Then answer these questions: "Is this the kind of person I want to be? Are these the things I really want to be spending my time doing?"

The Myers-Briggs

Many of you have taken a Myers-Briggs assessment. It was developed in the dark days of World War II when it was necessary to assess large numbers of people quickly in order to position them in the best jobs for their personality.

It is not a test, but an indicator of character type. There are four areas to it, with two possible orientations. The different combinations yield sixteen character types. To give you a brief idea where you stand, do the following exercise. While this does not replace the standard test (which can be found online or in the book *Please Understand Me: Character and Temperament Type*), the exercise can put you in the ballpark for our purposes:

Exercise 18: CHARACTER

Pick A or B for each of the four areas that best describe you:

AREA 1

Block A	**Block B**
Act first, think later?	Think first, then act?
Feel deprived if cut off from world?	Need private time to get energized?

Motivated by outside world?	Internally motivated?
Get energized by groups?	Groups drain your energy?

AREA 2

Block A	**Block B**
Mentally live in the now?	Mentally live in the future?
Use common sense for practical solutions?	Use imagination for innovative solutions?
Memory focuses on details and facts?	Memory focuses on patterns and context?
Don't like guessing?	Like guessing?

AREA 3

Block A	**Block B**
Search for facts to make a decision?	Go with feelings to make a decision?
Notice work to be accomplished?	Focus on people's needs?
Tend to provide an objective analysis?	Seek consensus and popular opinion?
Believe conflict is all right?	Dislike conflict and avoid it at all costs?

AREA 4

Block A	**Block B**
Plan detail before taking action?	Are comfortable taking action without a plan?
Complete tasks in order?	Like to multitask?
Stay ahead of deadlines?	Work best close to deadlines?
Set goals, deadlines, and routines?	Like to be flexible and avoid commitments?

THE RESULTS:

1A = Extrovert (E)	1B = Introvert (I)
2A = Sensing (S)	2B = iNtuition (N)
3A = Thinking (T)	3B = Feeling (F)
4A = Judging (J)	4B = Perceiving (P)

(*continued on next page*)

List out your four letters. You are one of sixteen Myers-Briggs character types:

INTP = Architect	ESFJ = Seller
ENTP = Inventor	ISFJ = Conservator
INTJ = Scientist	ESFP = Entertainer
ENTJ = Field Marshal	ISFP = Artist
INFP = Questor	ESTJ = Administrator
ENFP = Journalist	ISTJ = Trustee
INFJ = Author	ESTP = Promoter
ENFJ = Pedagogue	ISTP = Artisan

The first letter is extroversion versus introversion. This is how you view the world. E's are social while I's are territorial. E's prefer breadth and variety while I's prefer depth and one-on-one. E's tend to be externally motivated while I's tend to be internally motivated. Seventy-five percent of people are E's, while twenty-five percent are I's.

The second letter is iNtuition versus Sensation. N's tend to be innovative while S's are practical. This area is the greatest source of misunderstanding between people. Twenty-five percent of people are N's while seventy-five percent are S's.

The third letter is Thinking versus Feeling. T's analyze and decide in a detached manner, while F's analyze and decide in an emotional manner. Basically T's are logical while F's are emotional. The population is split fifty-fifty, but overall more women are Feeling and more men are Thinking.

The fourth letter is Judging versus Perceiving. J's like closure while P's like things open-ended. J's like the result while P's like the process. The population is fifty-fifty in this factor too.

Looking at your character type can give you an idea of yourself. It shows you how you interact with other people, how you take in information, how you make decisions, how you view processes.

It is very important to look at what the exact opposite of your character type is, and you'll get an idea of your blind spots and your weaknesses. I learned this as a writer.

CHARACTER: THE ARTIST'S IMAGINATION

I began my second career as an author by being a plot-driven writer. It took me ten years and a lot of hard work before I saw that I was going about things the wrong way. In the same way that in Special Forces we put people first, a writer has to do the same thing in novels—put the characters first.

People relate more to people, not things.

Think about your favorite novel. What do you remember the most? It is most likely the characters, not the plot. When writing a novel, I want my main character to have "arc." This means the character changes—just like you will change by implementing the tools in this book.

In a novel, if you thrust the main character into the climactic scene without having him change from the beginning of the novel, the character should fail. The journey that character goes through in the story should change him, so that when he faces the antagonist in the climactic scene, the main character will win.

The same change will be required in your life, if you want to succeed in the critical moments you committed yourself to facing when you set your goals. You must step out of your comfort zone and do things that are inherently against your nature so you can conquer fear and succeed.

Another enlightening experience for me was to look at the Myers-Briggs types (I was an INFJ—author) and noting what the exact opposite type, ESTP, was: promoter. This made me see some of my blind spots and forced me to work to get out of my comfort zone and into my fear zone to promote my books and business. It also required me to ask for assistance in areas I was weak in.

By the way, the exercises you've done in this tool are the same exercises I use to develop characters for a novel.

WHAT IS *CHANGE*
AND HOW DO YOU DO IT?

INTRODUCTION

"In war everything is simple, but even the simple is difficult."

—CARL VON CLAUSEWITZ

If you aren't where you want to be, then you must change. How many people do you know who have really changed? Your answer will ultimately depend on what you think *Change* is.

I can tell you what change isn't: change is not simply thinking differently. Thinking doesn't change anything in the world outside of your mind. Here comes my next paradox, though—the first step of change is to think differently. Note, I say it is the first step.

An official definition of change is to make or become different. There's a big difference between the verbs *make* and *become*. It's the difference between being ordinary and being successful:

- *Make* is externally imposed.
- *Become* is internally motivated.

The successful become.

Can people change? If the answer to that is no, then there is no purpose to this book and we all might as well quit now. There's good news, though—history has proven that people *can* change. Change is very difficult, and very few people manage to achieve great change in their lives and sustain it. These people are the successful ones.

SPECIAL FORCES ASSESSMENT AND SELECTION THOUGHT:
To become is hard; to be is even harder.

BLOOD LESSON: FROM SCHOLAR TO WARRIOR TO SCHOLAR TO POLITICIAN

"But we can hold our spirits and our bodies so pure and high, we may cherish such thoughts and ideals, and dream such dreams of lofty purpose, that we can determine and know what manner of men we will be, whenever and wherever the hour strikes and calls to noble action."

—JOSHUA CHAMBERLAIN

The problem

The Civil War was fought primarily by volunteers. At the start of the war there were only 1,080 regular army officers. There was an urgent need for officers as the army exploded in size. Where did these men come from? How could one change from doing a civilian job to becoming a military officer commanding thousands of soldiers in combat? How could one man make the radical change from seminary professor to soldier?

The solution

Officers were found in many places, but they were mostly political appointees. Some units even elected their own officers. Since

most new officers had little or no military background, there were
no guidelines to appoint people on merit.

An officer who made one of the greatest changes from civilian
life to military life, and commanded the most strategic position at
the pivotal battle of Gettysburg—perhaps enabling the Union to
eventually win the war—was Lawrence Joshua Chamberlain from
Maine.

Chamberlain was given the name Lawrence in honor of Com-
modore James Lawrence, who said, "Don't give up the ship!"
while battling the British during the War of 1812. His parents had
great foresight, because Chamberlain would take those words to
heart later in life, not at sea, but on a small hill in southern Penn-
sylvania.

As a child working the rough fields of Maine, he learned that
strength of character, followed by sustained willpower in action,
could bring about change. His father wanted him to go to the Military Academy at West Point, while his mother preferred for him
to study for the ministry—a rather wide gulf between possible career paths. Mother prevailed when Chamberlain entered Bowdoin
College. Perhaps as a sign of his change in path, he began using
Joshua as his first name, dropping the military-heritage first name.
As a student, he earned a reputation for sticking to his principles,
even when challenged by authority.

After graduating, Chamberlain took a position teaching rhet-
oric and oratory at Bowdoin. When the Civil War broke out, he
wanted to enlist, but the Bowdoin College administration felt he
was too valuable to be given permission to do this. They granted
him a leave of absence to study language abroad in Europe for
two years. Chamberlain left the school and promptly enlisted.

He was offered command of the 20th Maine but declined,

saying he needed to "start a little lower and learn the business first." He was appointed a lieutenant colonel and served under a recent West Point graduate to learn how to be an officer. Chamberlain learned so well, he eventually *earned* command of the 20th Maine, leading to his fateful encounter with destiny.

On July 2, 1863, the 20th Maine was put in position on the far left flank of the Union Army at Gettysburg. Chamberlain was ordered to hold a hill, Little Round Top, at all costs. He did so until his unit's ammunition was nearly depleted and his men exhausted.

Chamberlain then did something one would least expect in such dire straits: he ordered his men to fix bayonets and attack. So stunning was this move that the equally exhausted Confederate soldiers, who had been attacking all day, broke. Chamberlain had saved the left flank—and the Union Army.

In April 1864, Chamberlain was so severely wounded in battle that General Grant gave him a posthumous promotion to brigadier general. The posthumous part was a bit premature, since Chamberlain survived his wound. Chamberlain fought in twenty battles and numerous skirmishes, was cited for bravery four times, had six horses shot from under him, and was wounded six times. He'd come a long way from being the ministry student.

At the end of the war, when Lee surrendered to Grant at Appomattox, Grant selected Chamberlain to preside over the formal surrender parade of Confederate infantry. As the defeated Confederates marched by to lay down their arms and colors, Chamberlain had his men come to attention and present arms as a sign of respect. The Confederate commander in turn had his men return the gesture. The seeds of reconciliation were sown by these simple, respectful gestures, initiated by a former ministry student

and college professor who had evolved into one of the best officers in the Union Army.

After the war, Chamberlain, bored with the academic life and
much changed by his wartime experiences, ran for governor of
Maine and won by the largest majority in the state's history. He
served four consecutive terms.

The lesson

Thirty years after the end of the Civil War, Chamberlain was
awarded the Medal of Honor for his actions on Little Round Top.

Here's the text of his citation: *"Daring heroism and great
tenacity in holding his position on the Little Round Top against
repeated assaults, and carrying the advance position on the Great
Round Top."*

Simple and to the point, just like the man.

Because Joshua Chamberlain was willing to learn and change
his actions, he achieved great things as a scholar, a soldier, and a
statesman.

But how exactly did he change?

THE THREE STEPS OF CHANGE

There are three steps of change:

1. You have a *moment of enlightenment.*
2. You make a *decision* to take a different course of action from what
    you have been doing.
3. Commitment to your decision leads to *sustained action,* which
    brings about permanent change.

Joshua Chamberlain went through these three steps en route to becoming one of the greatest leaders of the Civil War. Let's look at both the fundamental character and situational changes for him.

Fundamental character change:

Moment of Enlightenment: When war broke out, as an avowed abolitionist and Federalist, Chamberlain realized he had to take action in support of his beliefs.

Decision: Instead of going to Europe, he enlisted.

Sustained Action: Realizing he didn't have the expertise to command right away, he apprenticed himself to a more experienced officer, learning the skills needed to command.

Situational change:

Moment of Enlightenment: When the 20th Maine was about to be overrun, he realized that the attacking forces had to be as exhausted and as close to collapse as his own men.

Decision: He gave the order to charge, when most other officers would have given the order to retreat.

Sustained Action: Chamberlain personally led the charge, making sure the men of Maine defeated the Confederates who were assaulting his position and straightened out the Union line for a better defensive position.

Moment of enlightenment

Most of what you do day in and day out is out of habit. And habits are extremely difficult to change. To have a moment of enlightenment, you have to become open-minded, one of the character traits we've already talked about. You have to be able to change your point of view—your perspective. You must get out of your everyday rut.

Break out of your comfort zone and look at something in the opposite way from how you've always looked at it. Entertain the possibility that what you think is your greatest strength might actually be a defense (a blind spot) layered over your greatest flaw and might be blinding you to opportunities to change. Reverse thinking is a very strong tool to help find moments of enlightenment.

An example

A simple moment of enlightenment for me came in the Special Forces Qualification Course. During a patrolling exercise, we spent several February days being rained on—not exactly the most comfortable experience. Several students had to be medevacked out because of hypothermia. When the exercise concluded, we were given an eight-hour break, still out in the middle of the woods, before moving on to the next training exercise. We no longer had to be on alert.

It was still pouring and cold. Most students huddled, shivering and sopping wet, underneath their ponchos. I watched, though, as one student ignored the elements and walked about, gathering firewood. He piled it up, and then worked hard to get a fire started. After quite a bit of effort, he had a roaring blaze and a grateful circle of students standing around, warming themselves and drying off.

My moment of enlightenment? When miserable, don't just hunker down and ignore the environment—instead, take action to make the situation better. Over the years since, that simple realization has served me well in numerous situations. Thinking about being warm and dry while wet and cold did nothing. A decision was required, followed by a course of action—in this example, literally going against the elements.

Ways to have moments of enlightenment

Moments of enlightenment come in several ways:

- A new experience you've never encountered before affects you.
- Something you've experienced before affects you in a new way.
- You witness someone else doing something differently, and it affects you.

A successful person is always looking at the world around him, trying to uncover previously unseen possibilities. The more information you gather, the more possible courses of action you have.

Many times, those who surround us are trying to give us the gift of enlightenment, but we ignore their message. In a marriage, often one partner is trying to give the spouse enlightenment, but the message is ignored. At work, a co-worker might be pointing something out to you, which goes by you without your noticing. Sometimes, if you just listen to *yourself*, you're subconsciously trying to give yourself a MOE. When you finish this book, you'll be directed to go back and reread the answers you've written down for the exercises. Read them with an open mind and see what you're *really* saying in your answers.

Exercise 19: CHANGE

Fold a piece of paper in thirds. On the left third, write down three moments of enlightenment you've had since beginning this book.

Make a decision

Your moment of enlightenment is internal. So is the decision you must make next. If you don't make a decision to change, your moment of enlightenment will be gone—worthless.

In Area One, you learned that making a decision involves a succinct statement of what it is you want to achieve. It's important to write your decision—your goal—down. This is the first external action in the process of change.

Exercise 20: CHANGE

Using the paper from Exercise 19, in the middle column, write down a decision to change based on each of the three moments of enlightenment.

Chart a sustained course of action

Don't expect immediate, life-altering change as soon as you've made your decision. While this does happen, it is very rare.

Change is a slow process that requires dedication and commitment and, most of all, sustained action.

I've had varied teaching experiences: Special Forces team, JFK Special Warfare Center, master's degree classes in education, martial arts, writing, universities, conferences, organizations, etc. I can't count the number of times I've heard someone say: "I always wanted to write a book, but . . ." "I always wanted to get a black belt, but . . ." "I was going to try out for Special Forces, but . . ."

The successful don't do *but*'s. The successful are not wannabes. They learn. They decide. They act. They sustain the action.

Train for change

The military is very big on training because it wants to change people from civilians into soldiers. The goal of Special Forces training is to change regular soldiers into elite warriors. You can use some of the Special Forces training templates to achieve sustained change in your life.

The history of Special Forces Assessment and Selection (SFAS) goes back to the formation of Delta Force, and before that back to the British SAS. SFAS was created in an attempt to learn from history and from others who'd already done what Special Forces needed to do.

According to official doctrine, SFAS tests an applicant's tactical skills, leadership, physical fitness, motivation, and ability to cope with stress. This is done through overland movements, psychological tests, physical fitness tests, swim tests, runs, obstacle courses, small unit tactics exercises, land navigation exercises, and individual and team problem solving.

Aspiring Special Forces soldiers coming to the course are advised that their mind is their best weapon, that being physically fit isn't enough to get them through. Applicants should be prepared for anything.

In this type of training, expectations are unclear. There are unknown variables and standards. This places students under stress—as you've already learned, an excellent evaluation technique to see if someone can be successful. I've seen students become so frustrated that they quit.

There's none of the harassment or "false" stress that's used in many training situations. Once you've been through a "getting screamed in your face" training environment, the second time you experience it, the effect is almost ludicrous. When you are testing the elite, the stress has to be real. Focus on the times in your life when the stress was real and examine your actions.

Goal-aligned training programs

Just as your goals must be aligned to support one another, your training plans must be goal-aligned. Often you have many things you want to achieve. You must prioritize your goals, both primary and subordinate—again, in writing. When designing your personal training programs, this priority must be clearly understood, so your time is well spent and your training for one goal doesn't become counterproductive to another.

Goal alignment must happen every day. As a writer, when I start a new book, I post my one-sentence original idea on my desk and read it every day to keep myself on task and avoid going off on tangents.

As a martial arts student and then instructor, I learned that the key to success, as is the case in many other training fields, is repetition. You have to do the same kick again and again and again—correctly—until one day, after thousands and thousands of kicks, the motion becomes instinctual. Sustained action changes habits.

In Ranger school, the proper response to an ambush is drilled into students day after day—because it goes against your survival instinct to charge into an attacking force. Repetition is the key to both training and aiming for the right goal at the right time. Follow your goal-aligned training plan every day—do it right every day—and sooner or later you will achieve a new habit to replace the one you want to change.

Scientists have found that while you can't "unprogram" the neural pathways that form your habits, you can build detours around bad habits by building parallel neural pathways. The more you sustain the new habit, the stronger that pathway becomes, and the less power the old habit holds.

Exercise 21: CHANGE

For each decision to change you listed in Exercise 20, in the right column, define the sustained action you would have to do to achieve the change you desire.

Focus your training program on yourself, not other people.

If you've read this far into *Who Dares Wins*, you're searching for something. You want to change things in your life. One of the most dangerous phases in change is when you realize you're not where you want to be, but then look outward for the reasons, looking for someone or something else to be at fault. This is especially true in relationships, where we tend to think changing the other person will improve the relationship.

The only person you can change is yourself. Trying to change another person will often bring about more negative results than positive. Learn from those who have something you want. Ask for help when you need it. Try to be open to that which at first doesn't seem to make sense or fit. A successful individual focuses on changing himself—which is a very long-term process.

Training is action. Doing. Not talking about doing. The bottom line comes down to doing the hard work of sustained action, and rigorously evaluating your results.

Some of the hardest courses in the military involve no harassment, no screaming, no yelling. Elite courses stay focused on achieving set standards. When I led my team through Danish Scout Swim School, we were simply told on the first day what was required to graduate:

- Swim thirty meters underwater.
- Free-dive ten meters down.
- Do a ten-kilometer surface swim within a certain time.
- Do a one-kilometer surface swim within a certain time.
- Successfully complete the school's obstacle course.
- Tie three knots around a pipe while submerged.

Then we spent several weeks practicing these events along with other training. The instructors simply told us what to do each day, and we did it. And it was very, very hard.

Set your evaluation standards the same way you set goals: phrase them in the form of a single sentence, and write them down. Then follow through. Day after day.

Exercise 22: CHANGE

Using your goal-aligned training program from Exercises 19–21, list the standards you need to meet to achieve sustained change. Post these standards where you can see them every day. Make the standards external goals that can clearly be assessed—you either achieve the standard or you don't.

FIVE PERCENT

The successful are the top five percent.

Why did I settle on that number? Because studies—and my experiences as a Special Forces soldier, best-selling author, writing instructor, and martial arts instructor—have shown that approximately five percent of people are capable of internally motivated, sustained change. Yes, certainly some people are born with unique gifts and talents, but the successful decide to take the road less traveled and stay the course.

It's difficult to go against the norm, to challenge most people's perceptions about how life should be lived. But to be successful, you must resist the pull of the ninety-five percent of people who live in fear—and with mediocrity.

Who Dares Wins **tools help you successfully function against the norm.**

CHANGE: THE ARTIST'S IMAGINATION

Ninety-five percent of the students I've worked with as a writing instructor have not really improved as writers. Perhaps it reflects on my abilities as a teacher. But I also found ninety-five percent of the students I worked with as a martial arts instructor did not reach black belt level. When I was a teacher at the JFK Special Warfare Center and School, the success rate was somewhat higher, about thirty percent, but these were highly motivated volunteers who'd already been through several screening processes.

It's reported that eighty-two percent of Americans believe they can write a book. The actual number that actually start writing a book is much lower. The percentage that manage to produce a completed manuscript is far lower, down in the single digits.

Whatever you want to achieve, whatever you want to be, the only solution is to actually do it—by taking action every day to get one step closer to your goal.

In writing, I learned that this was called "bum glue"—gluing my bum to a chair every day, sitting at the computer, and actually writing. All my great dreams, my wonderful thoughts, all of that was worthless if I didn't sit down and actually put words on the page.

A writer by definition must write. Whatever it is you want to achieve must be externalized into action, not left to thought, where it will wither away until it's worthless.

For you to be successful, change must become a way of life.

HOW DO YOU BUILD
THE *COURAGE* TO CHANGE?

INTRODUCTION

There are several definitions of courage:

- The state or quality of mind or spirit that enables one to face danger with self-possession, confidence, and resolution.
- The ability to do something that frightens one.
- Strength in the face of pain or grief.

The dictionary also tells us that fear is a feeling of alarm or disquiet caused by the expectation of danger, pain, disaster, etc. Since courage is taking action in the face of fear, this means you must:

1. Accept that your fears are part of your character.
2. Understand that what you really fear—often your blind spot—is something you are often unaware of, but have begun to look at after Tool Four.
3. Determine what actions you must take to overcome your fear in your decision-making, rather than ignoring it.
4. Train to overcome fear through sustained action.
5. Prepare for the things you fear the most in order to reduce the fear.

SPECIAL FORCES ASSESSMENT AND SELECTION THOUGHT:
Strength is proven in adversity.

BLOOD LESSON: THE MEN WHO DID

Heroism is acting in the face of fear.

The problem

On Sunday, October 3, 1993, a Blackhawk helicopter was shot down in Mogadishu, Somalia. An armed mob was closing in on the downed helicopter and its crew. The only American forces in the vicinity were two elite Delta Force operatives flying overhead in another chopper.

The solution

Sergeants Shughart and Gordon requested permission to secure and rescue the men from the downed Blackhawk. Being professional soldiers and having watched the situation unfold, they knew that the grounded soldiers had slim odds of holding off that mob until additional help arrived.

The sergeants repeatedly volunteered for a mission no one had ordered them to do, in a country none of them had any stake in. To rescue men they weren't even sure were alive and did not personally know. On a mission dictated from half a world away, with nebulous goals that were constantly changing at the National Command Authority level.

In the same situation, an ordinary person would not have made such a request, or when the request was granted, wouldn't have jumped from the hovering helicopter, knowing the advancing mob was getting closer.

But these sergeants were not ordinary people—Sergeants

Shughart and Gordon were Special Operations forces. They were the elite. Being courageous in the face of fear was their state of mind.

Why did they do this? How were their actions different from the way most others would have reacted? What made them elite?

Here is the Medal of Honor citation for Master Sergeant Gordon:

"Rank and organization: Master Sergeant, U.S. Army. Place and date: 3 October 1993, Mogadishu, Somalia. Born: Lincoln, Maine. Citation: Master Sergeant Gordon, United States Army, distinguished himself by actions above and beyond the call of duty on 3 October 1993, while serving as Sniper Team Leader, United States Army Special Operations Command with Task Force Ranger in Mogadishu, Somalia.

"Master Sergeant Gordon's sniper team provided precision fires from the lead helicopter during an assault and at two helicopter crash sites, while subjected to intense automatic weapons and rocket-propelled grenade fires. When Master Sergeant Gordon learned that ground forces were not immediately available to secure the second crash site, he and another sniper unhesitatingly volunteered to be inserted to protect the four critically wounded personnel, despite being well aware of the growing number of enemy personnel closing in on the site.

"After his third request to be inserted, Master Sergeant Gordon received permission to perform his volunteer mission. When debris and enemy ground fires at the site caused them to abort the first attempt, Master Sergeant Gordon was inserted one hundred meters south of the crash site.

"Equipped with only his sniper rifle and a pistol, Master Sergeant Gordon and his fellow sniper, while under intense small arms fire

from the enemy, fought their way through a dense maze of shanties and shacks to reach the critically injured crew members. Master Sergeant Gordon immediately pulled the pilot and the other crew members from the aircraft, establishing a perimeter which placed him and his fellow sniper in the most vulnerable position. Master Sergeant Gordon used his long-range rifle and side arm to kill an undetermined number of attackers until he depleted his ammunition. Master Sergeant Gordon then went back to the wreckage, recovering some of the crew's weapons and ammunition.

"Despite the fact that he was critically low on ammunition, he provided some of it to the dazed pilot and then radioed for help. Master Sergeant Gordon continued to travel the perimeter, protecting the downed crew. After his team member was fatally wounded and his own rifle ammunition exhausted, Master Sergeant Gordon returned to the wreckage, recovering a rifle with the last five rounds of ammunition, and gave it to the pilot with the words 'good luck.' Then, armed only with his pistol, Master Sergeant Gordon continued to fight until he was fatally wounded.

"His actions saved the pilot's life. Master Sergeant Gordon's extraordinary heroism and devotion to duty were in keeping with the highest standards of military service and reflect great credit upon him, his unit, and the United States Army."

The lesson

Shughart and Gordon were heroes. They took an action to help their comrades, despite their fear. The sergeants were able to take the action because they had the necessary character and training, because they had a primary motivator that allowed them to overcome their fear. While this is another extreme example, the things you face in your life are important to you. There are many events that will cause you to dig deep and find the courage to face them.

FEAR AND YOUR BLIND SPOT

We all have a blind spot, a part of our personality that is hidden from ourselves. Often, it is this blind spot that keeps us from being successful. And the majority of the time this blind spot is rooted in our deepest fears.

Remember, your strongest emotional defenses are built around your greatest emotional weaknesses. Special Operations training is brutal and direct, because it's designed to drill down to a person's character weaknesses—his blind spot—without the benefit of a therapist's light touch.

It is critical to find your blind spot and the first step in that is . . .

Honesty with yourself

Honesty plays a key role in being successful. The only way to uncover your blind spot is to be honest with yourself, and honest with those who want to help you. It is amazing that often people pay large amounts of money to see a therapist, walk into the session, and then lie, defeating the entire purpose of what they are paying for.

In the beginning of this book, in Exercise 1, I asked you to write down what you feared the most. Odds are, your blind spot is affiliated with that fear somehow. However, your defenses are so good that often your blind spot is the exact opposite of what you'd describe as your greatest strength. Sometimes it could even be what you view as your greatest strength, because it might actually be your greatest defense and thus very powerful.

There are tools to help you understand your character and fears, and to learn to be courageous as you face them. We already discussed looking at the character traits that are opposite to yours, as outlined in the Myers-Briggs character assessment test. Another way is to examine your strengths and see where the potential blind spot might be, using the . . .

Traits, needs, flaws paradigm

This paradigm takes a character trait, defines the need associated with it, and illustrates the potential flaw you'll face dealing with that part of your character.

Every character trait is double-edged: there is both a positive and a negative potential. A good way to delve deeper into your blind spot, to understand your true nature, is to look at what you consider your character strength—then find the need driving that strength, and then the corresponding weakness or flaw you are less comfortable looking at when you push that need to an extreme.

For example, consider these character traits, needs, and corresponding character flaws (blind spots):

CHARACTER TRAIT	NEED	POTENTIAL FLAW
Loyal	To be trusted	Gullible
Adventurous	To change	Unreliable
Altruistic	To be loved	Submissive
Tolerant	To have no conflict	No conviction
Decisive	To be in charge	Impetuous

Realistic	To be balanced	Controlled by events
Competitive	To achieve goals	Overlook costs
Idealistic	To find/achieve the best	Naïve

Exercise 23: COURAGE

In one word, record what you believe to be your greatest character trait (the list above is not a complete one).

Exercise 24: COURAGE

Using that trait, write down the corresponding need and potential flaw (blind spot).

Everyone wants to succeed, but most people succumb to the enemy—fear:

- Fear of failure
- Fear of lack of security
- Fear of success—which can be the most insidious and hardest fear to identify

Most fear is subconscious. Fear is a fact of life, but it can become debilitating if not faced and dealt with. It is likely at the core of most of the day-to-day problems you face.

For example, in uncertain times, when business is bad and layoffs threaten, a tremendous amount of energy can be wasted by employees worrying about job security—rather than accomplishing their team's mission. This can lead to a negative spiral of defeat and failure. There is such a thing as a self-fulfilling prophecy.

When fear becomes too great, the emotion itself can bring about what is feared.

When you begin to panic, you expend energy that should be used to avert whatever it is that you fear. Are you willing to let the hidden enemy predetermine your failure or success at achieving your goal?

Exercise 25: COURAGE

Describe the last time you wanted to do something you knew was the right thing to do, but you didn't do it. What kept you from doing it?

While your answer might be something mundane such as laziness or lack of time, peel away those reasons and search for the fear underneath.

It's not uncommon to design your life based on your hidden fears (blind spots), creating your own bunker—which is more a cave to hide in than a courageous place from which to succeed at your goals.

If fear prevents you from committing to achieving your goals, your failure is ensured by your own hand—a self-fulfilling prophecy.

Exercise 26: COURAGE

Based on what you've uncovered in this tool and under *Character*, list those traits, needs, and flaws that you feel compromise your character. Then list the fears (blind spots) that you suspect hurt you.

Fear is not a total negative. Two of the primary reasons why this emotion exists—that you can use to your advantage—are to serve as a warning (when you're in danger) and as an indicator (sometimes, of exactly what you need to do).

Fear as a warning

We fear things because we believe they are threats to us. And sometimes things *do* threaten us. So to toss fear on the scrap heap opens us up to getting hurt—not the same thing as the pain that can come with positive change.

You've heard people talk about sixth sense. I believe sixth sense is the power of the subconscious taking care of us—a part of our mind that combines signals from the five senses, and warns us when something we don't consciously see, touch, smell, taste, or hear is a real threat.

A point man on a military patrol should have excellent sixth sense. For example, a good point man's eyes might notice something—a broken twig, a trip wire—that his mind doesn't consciously process. But his subconscious, which is also processing information, sends a warning to the conscious mind in the form of the emotion of fear. Of course, he must be tuned in to his indicators to recognize the trigger, and act on the basis of his fear.

You should pay attention to vague feelings of unease or fear. Don't ignore these feelings, because sometimes they are indications of real trouble. If you get "bad vibes" from a person or a situation, focus on it. This is part of developing your elite character traits.

After something bad has happened to you, how many times do you look back and realize there were warning signs that you ignored?

Exercise 27: COURAGE

Think back to the last really bad thing that happened to you. Write it down. Then write down the warning signs that were present before it happened, but that you didn't focus on.

These warning signs are fear indicators that you should write down and post so that you can see them every day. Read them, focus on them, and determine if they are coming up again with regard to something else in your life.

Just like your anger flash points tell you something about yourself, your fear indicators are important character traits to learn. The wall of fear is the demarcation line between being ordinary and being successful. Ordinary people live lives filled with fear, cut off from positive action because of it. Successful people have fear, but act toward their desired goals in spite of it, constantly pushing their wall of courage further outward.

Fear can often indicate exactly what you need to do in order to succeed and the direction in which you need to push your courage. Yes, the fear is a warning that you could fail. But remember— if you don't try, you can never succeed. And you'll never know your true fear threshold if you're not willing to challenge it.

EXPAND YOUR COMFORT ZONE BY VENTURING INTO YOUR COURAGE ZONE

The best way to overcome fear is to prepare for it. To train for it. You have a comfort zone, and around that you have a courage zone. Most people rarely venture into their courage zone because of fear. Successful people venture into their courage zones often. By doing so, they expand their comfort zone and push the boundaries of both their comfort and courage zones further and further—this is conquering fear and becoming successful.

We cannot think ourselves through change; we must make the decision to start change. Then, take action. No one ever got a Medal of Honor for thinking about doing something heroic. Training is repetitive action. It is the key to overcoming fear because it builds your confidence. We talked about this in the previous tool: Change.

Remaining inside your comfort zone ensures you will never grow. Straining the boundaries of what you are used to makes becoming a better and stronger person possible.

The number of airborne-qualified soldiers in the Army far exceeds the number of airborne slots. Why does the Army send so many more people, particularly officers, through airborne training than it needs?

At the introduction to ground week, the first of three distinct phases of training, you're told that it's not normal to jump out of a perfectly functioning airplane. In fact, it goes against a person's ingrained survival instincts. And when survival is threatened, the normal reaction is fear.

Short of actually shooting at trainees, airborne school is one of the Army's ways to put a large number of soldiers in a high-stress situation and make them take an action directly in the face of the fear—throwing themselves out of an airplane door at fifteen hundred feet. To be successful, you must face fear. You must train to act in a positive, targeted manner in the face of it, moving you closer to achieving your goals.

I'm not just talking about physical conflict. Mental stress can take a significant toll. In West Point's Beast Barracks, physical hazing is prohibited. Yet plebes are under stress the entire time, due to mental pressure and the requirement to perform, to act, despite it. Train for fear by regularly performing under pressure. You don't really know someone until you see them act in a crisis. Don't wait until a real crisis to know your reaction to the unexpected.

How do you expand your comfort zone?

Do something *positive* you don't want to do—something that expands your comfort zone as you repeatedly go into your courage zone:

- If you're typically introverted, make yourself approach and talk to a complete stranger every day.
- If you're a practical person, force yourself to make a minor decision intuitively.
- Have you ever spent a night by yourself outdoors?
- Have you ever sat still for just one hour doing nothing—no TV, no music, no book. Just by yourself? Looking inward?

Practice facing your blind spots, regularly acting to achieve the goals your hidden fears are blocking.

Exercise 28: COURAGE

Based on your answer to Exercise 26, pick one flaw and write down one positive act that would challenge you to face that blind spot, act in the face of fear, and enter your courage zone.

Exercise 29: COURAGE

For the next week, do this one positive act every day. By the end of the week, your comfort zone will have expanded.

CATASTROPHE PLANNING TO REDUCE FEAR AND INCREASE SUCCESS

A technique we used in Special Forces was to do worst-case scenarios and plan for dealing with potential catastrophes. There were two major reasons for this: first, because planning for the worst case saves lives, and second, because planning for dealing with catastrophe reduces fear and allows you to focus more of your energy on positive success, instead of worrying about "What if things go wrong?" because you've already answered the question in your catastrophe planning.

Take any situation you might face and worst-case it. What will you do if that worst case happens? If you don't have a plan already in place, you need to make one—because your subconscious knows you don't have a plan and it keeps you in a constant state of tension and worry, sapping the strength you need to be successful.

Exercise 30: COURAGE

Fold a piece of paper in half, and on the left side, for the following areas, write down a potential catastrophe that could occur:

Physical

Financial

Natural disaster

Work

Relationship

The next major task you have to do

For example, look at where you live. Are you in a hurricane zone? An earthquake zone? A tsunami zone? Forest fire area? Do you have a plan already in place and are you prepared to execute it in case the worst happens? If you live in a house that is below sea level in a city that relies on levees to keep the sea at bay, do you have a plan in place in case the levees fail? If you live in a hurricane area, do you have your important papers, pictures, keepsakes, food, supplies, and so forth already packed and ready to be loaded? Do you have spare gas cans filled up and ready to be taken? Do you have a checklist you can refer to in case of evacuation so you don't forget to do something important, like turn the gas off?

It's too late to make these plans once the catastrophe occurs.

Exercise 31: COURAGE

On the right side of the paper from Exercise 30, write out your plan in case the catastrophe occurs and make the necessary preparations.

COURAGE: THE ARTIST'S IMAGINATION

As a writer, I've learned to trust my subconscious. I warn new writers not to edit themselves too harshly while writing a novel—their subconscious will put things into the manuscript that they won't consciously recognize the immediate need for but that will serve an important purpose later on. I teach writers to trust that the part of their mind they don't consciously control is working for them, planting seeds that will be reaped later on.

In the same way, paying attention to fears in your life that don't make much sense now, facing them with courage and training to deal with your indicators, will pay off in huge dividends later.

Writing fiction is an extremely precarious occupation in terms of security. I advise new writers to catastrophe plan—have a backup plan in case writing doesn't work out. Not because I don't think it will work out for them, but so they don't waste their creative energy worrying and focus on their writing. Writers who constantly live in fear of not getting the next book contract eventually break down—and don't get another contract.

Courage is a state of mind.

Courage is acknowledging fear, then taking action in the face of it. The more you do this, the more success you will achieve.

WHO, THE GREEN BERET WAY

INTRODUCTION

Who Dares Wins tools help you change the way you're living. A key to the Circle of Success is understanding yourself, particularly your blind spots, uncovering the hidden fears that keep you mired in the mundane, then making decisions to act and train to be the successful you.

Change is a long-term, three-step process, ultimately requiring sustained action. But in the long run, trying to achieve your goals without understanding yourself and factoring in your fears is counterproductive.

A classic example of training that is counterproductive to mission accomplishment occurred during my plebe year at West Point. The Academy is designed to train leaders for the modern Army. Yet while I was there, some training was still rooted in archaic techniques. Plebes were expected to memorize large amounts of plebe knowledge. One of these was General Schofield's definition of discipline:

"The discipline which makes the soldiers of a free country reliable in battle is not to be gained by harsh or tyrannical treatment. On the contrary, such treatment is far more likely to destroy than to make an army."

I remember standing in the hallway of the barracks at West Point, braced against the wall by an upperclassman who would demand I recite the definition, as a form of hazing. There was an inherent contradiction between the content of what I was saying and the context under which I was saying it. Did this training result in daring, sustained change? Not compared to what I learned among the successful in Special Forces.

BLOOD LESSON: FROM REGULAR SOLDIER TO GUERRILLA LEADER

The problem

In 1941, Colonel Russell Volckman, a 1934 West Point graduate, was serving in the Philippines. At that time, an assignment to the Philippines was considered a plum posting. The exotic locale, low cost of living, and the opportunity to work under General Douglas MacArthur were all strong attractions to young graduates. The U.S. Army was still in World War I mode—it is said every army is always prepared to fight the last war, not the next one, because they aren't willing to change.

When the Japanese invaded the Philippines, Volckman and many other Americans were captured as the last stronghold, the Bataan Peninsula, fell.

The solution

Volckman did not accept his fate as a prisoner. The night before what was to become known as the Bataan Death March began, he and several other soldiers slipped under the wire and escaped into the jungle.

While General MacArthur snuck out of Bataan on a PT boat,

vowing "I will return," Volckman later wrote a book titled *We Remained*.

Volckman had no experience in unconventional warfare. If he had followed orders, he would have stayed a prisoner and gone on the Death March. If he had survived that, he would have spent the rest of the war imprisoned under horrible conditions.

His character was such, though, that he disobeyed orders and escaped. Then he began to learn a new way of fighting. Linking up with indigenous forces, he and the others who had escaped with him began a guerrilla warfare campaign against the Japanese that would last over three years.

Volckman had the courage to violate his order to surrender (Rule breaking—Tool Nine) and then to survive behind enemy lines for three years—not just to survive, but to learn how to conduct a style of warfare for which he'd had little training. He learned day-to-day, on the job.

He had a moment of enlightenment, made a decision, and conducted sustained action for three years. He displayed courage in the face of harsh conditions, day after day.

The result

The guerrilla forces in the Philippines became so effective that they tied down large parts of the Japanese army. These behind-the-lines fighters caused tremendous problems for the Japanese and helped ensure the success of the invasion, when MacArthur finally did return in 1944.

After World War II, Volckman, along with Colonel Aaron Banks, fought to establish a force that would be prepared to fight the next war behind the lines. When Volckman and Banks finally received the approval to establish a "special" unit that would conduct unconventional warfare—the beginning of Special Forces—they faced a daunting task.

How would they select and assess the soldiers who would be part of the unit? What kind of character should Special Forces soldiers have? They focused on those men who had expertise in guerrilla warfare, spoke foreign languages, and were independent thinkers who could operate on their own as well as be members of a team.

Then Banks devised a Special Forces training program, drawing on his experience and those of others like Volckman, to teach Special Forces soldiers their blood lessons. A training plan for teaching a soldier how to conquer fear was designed with very high standards for success.

This training has been refined over the years, to the point where the Army now has a program in which select individuals can go directly from Basic Training to Airborne School to Special Forces training. These individuals are changed from civilians to elite warriors over the course of the training program . . .

Just like you are changing as you read and study and work through each *Who Dares Wins* tool.

ALIGN CHARACTER, CHANGE, AND COURAGE—TO WIN!

You're now ready to pull together everything you've learned about *What*, *Why*, *Where*, *Character*, *Change*, and *Courage*. In the conclusion of Area One: Wins, I gave you my A-Team experience, and I've shared many other military examples and templates since. But as you've learned, Area Two: Who—and change—is all about you.

So, in this area's conclusion, I'm giving you a very important challenge:

To review the Circle of Success again and again—based on the work you've done so far and the work you've yet to do in Area Three: Dares—and then again, if needed. To keep reviewing and learning and changing your goals and decisions and training programs. To continue challenging yourself to be successful and to learn and to grow, as you master the tools of digging deeper into what you need and what you want and how you want to get it.

Let's take a look at what you've accomplished so far:

- You've recorded *What* you want to change and achieve. You've written these goals down, so you can track your progress and refine your intent as you learn and grow.
- You've recorded *Why* you want to achieve those goals.
- You've studied *Where* you will be achieving those goals and how achieving them will affect your environment.
- You've examined your *Character*, both your strengths and flaws. You've recorded the fears and blind spots that keep you from achieving your goals.
- You are using the three steps to *Change*.
- You are utilizing *Courage* to act in the face of fear and expand your courage zone.

Now it's time to take all you've learned and make these parts of the Circle of Success a way of life.

Your life.

It's time to read Area Three: Dares, to claim the successful life for your own.

AREA THREE

DARES

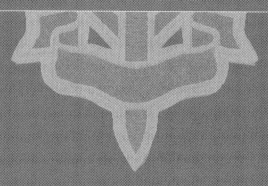

To complete the Circle of Success, to push yourself beyond
the ordinary, you must master personal *Communication*
and *Command*, and the daring it takes to *Complete*
everything you've learned, break rules, and win.

"Great spirits have always found violent opposition from mediocre minds. The latter cannot understand it when a man does not thoughtlessly submit to hereditary prejudices but honestly and courageously uses his intelligence and fulfills the duty to express the results of his thoughts in clear form."

—ALBERT EINSTEIN

What you've been learning up to now is the basics of the Green Beret way—the craft. Now it's time to graduate from learning craft to being an artist. It's time to separate from the norm, break rules, and *dare* to be different.

To succeed at being different, it is critical to have effective communication, master a command of self, and do a complete integration of all *Who Dares Wins* tools.

Because Special Forces are primarily teachers, effective communication skills are valued. Personal command is a core Special Forces trait. Every individual is expected to take charge and use initiative.

Integration of *Who Dares Wins* tools into your life takes you to another level, where you are then able to go back and refine your answers to the exercises in each of the various tools, making greater change and improving your way of life.

COMMUNICATE YOUR CHANGE
TO THE WORLD

INTRODUCTION

"Language grows out of life, out of its needs and experiences."

—ANNE SULLIVAN

The successful communicate clearly and effectively, so they can evoke a desired response and achieve their goals among others—family, co-workers, and friends.

Communication is essential to success: it is a large part of the way you interact with other people. It is a two-way street: you have to get your message across to others and receive the *true* messages others are sending.

The goal in communication is to be succinct, to be to the point, and to evoke a response.

SPECIAL FORCES ASSESSMENT AND SELECTION THOUGHT:
Defeat isn't bitter if you don't swallow it.

BLOOD LESSON: WHEN CAN THEIR GLORY FADE?

Miscommunication in battle gets people killed. A classic example of this is a military operation made famous by a poem written by Tennyson, "The Charge of the Light Brigade."

Without delving into the backstory explaining why the British were battling the Russians in the Crimea, suffice it to say that at a certain point in this war, the British found themselves facing the Russians at the Battle of Balaclava.

The problem

Lord Raglan, the commander of British army forces, sent a written order to the cavalry:

"Lord Raglan wishes the cavalry to advance rapidly to the front and to prevent the enemy carrying away the guns. Horse Artillery may accompany. French cavalry is on your left. Immediate."

The order was carried by an officer who was later killed, so it isn't known if there were further oral instructions to supplement this terse command. Nevertheless, when a successful leader issues a written order, he must make sure it can stand on its own.

"Attack what?" the cavalry commander asked the bearer.

The courier gestured vaguely. *"There, my Lord, is your enemy."*

The only guns the cavalry commander could see from his position were at the very end of the valley, over a mile away. And thus the fate of the Light Brigade was sealed.

In response to the order, the Earl of Cardigan led six hundred and seventy-three men straight into the valley between the Fediukhine Heights and the Causeway Heights. The Russians controlled not only the end of the valley toward which they were riding, but the heights on both sides. The Russians had over fifty artillery pieces and twenty battalions of infantry massed around this pocket of death. It was over a mile from the mouth of the valley to the Russian guns at the end, but Cardigan thought the guns were his objective and that was where he led his men.

As they galloped forward, the courier officer, realizing that the Light Brigade was heading down the valley instead of toward the closer Causeway Heights, which was the true objective, dashed forward on his horse, wildly waving his sword. He was obviously trying to let Cardigan know that they were going toward the wrong objective (albeit a bit late). However, as fate often has it, once things started going bad, they went from bad to worse.

The courier was struck by a fragment of a shell that killed him instantly. His sword fell from his hand, but his arm remained erect and the death grip of his knees kept him in the saddle. He galloped through the advancing Light Brigade, his true message dead with him.

The Russian artillery began to fire in earnest. Gaps opened in the Light Brigade lines as shot and shell swept through them. But they never paused nor stopped. The Russian infantry also began to fire, adding to the carnage. Still the Light Brigade charged on.

The survivors did reach the end of the valley and swept over the guns. So stunning was this attack that the Russian cavalry behind the guns, even though they far outnumbered the survivors of the Light Brigade, turned and ran despite the pleas of their officers.

However, the survivors among the Russian artillerymen manning the overrun guns began to fire again. The Russian cavalry regrouped and advanced, and all the Light Brigade could do now was retreat. There was no support from the rest of the British, because no one in the British lines knew what they had done, since it wasn't what they had been ordered to do.

The solution

When the smoke cleared, there were only one hundred and ninety-five men left. The stupidity combined with reckless bravery caused a French marshal to proclaim:

"It is magnificent, but it is not war."

On the Russian side, the commanders could only conclude that the British had been drunk.

> *When can their glory fade?*
> *O the wild charge they made!*
>   *All the world wonder'd.*
> *Honor the charge they made!*
> *Honor the Light Brigade,*
>   *Noble six hundred!*
>
> —TENNYSON

Nice poem.

Bad written order.

The lesson

As you write, keep in mind both your reader and the response that you desire.

Raglan, when he scribbled out his order, knew where he wanted the Light Brigade to attack. But since his point of view was different than Cardigan's—literally—he failed to specify the position. He failed to take into account the perspective of the recipient of the order he was issuing.

WHAT IS COMMUNICATION?

Communication is the means by which we exchange both information and emotion. It bridges the gap between inner thoughts and feelings and the external world. A successful person does not exist in a vacuum. Excellent communication is an essential skill. Communication is a two-way activity. Too many people focus on their ability to send a message and ignore their capability to receive information and read emotion in return. Focus on more than just the words.

> *Then farewell, Horace; whom I hated so,*
> *Not for thy faults, but mine. . . .*
>
> —LORD BYRON

When people communicate something that bothers you, realize you're having an emotional reaction because what was communicated, either verbally or nonverbally, resonated inside you. Fear plays a role in communication—we often fear being honest and react negatively to honesty from others.

Psychologists say only a small percentage of oral communication consists of actual words. Most information is transmitted through nonverbal cues. The phrase "read between the lines" is critical when dealing with written communication.

There are two primary forms of communication: written and oral. Another type of communication we've already discussed, although you might not have seen it that way, is action. We communicate very strongly through the actions we do.

Communication, in any form, is the key to interacting with other people.

WRITTEN COMMUNICATION

In my experience as a novelist, and having taught writing for two decades, I've found that approximately ninety-five percent of the people I've worked with don't communicate adequately with the written word. Note that we're once more back to that magic "successful" number of five percent.

I don't say this because the people I've worked with are incapable of written communication. They fail because they already think they *are* capable but are not willing to learn the craft of writing. They have a "fixed" mind-set, not a "growth" one. Becoming a successful writer, like becoming successful at anything else, is a skill that can be learned.

The key to good written communication is to not think like the writer, but to think like the reader.

The message in your head will be lost if you cannot express it well in writing. To be clear to your reader, your message has to develop in your reader's head. "The Charge of the Light Brigade" couldn't have illustrated this better, or more poignantly. You must make the reader's point of view a priority if your writing is to get the result you want.

Written communication makes thoughts real. As a writer I've had great thoughts, but when I attempt to write them down, they suddenly become ordinary. When you write, you are trying to transform something that is alive inside of your brain into something that is alive in the brain of your reader, through the sole medium of the printed word.

Written communication fixes responsibility

Writing things down clarifies your goals to others and assigns responsibility.

When your words are in black and white, you're putting your thoughts out there for others to see. While you should think like the reader when writing something, remember that responsibility for what you've written is always yours as the author.

Don't qualify. Don't write,

In my opinion . . .

Of course it's your opinion if you're writing it.

It appears that . . .

It either is or isn't. Of course it's filtered through your perception, so it appears that way to you.

Qualifiers are the written way of trying to distance yourself from what you're writing. You may be doing this subconsciously. But, remember, responsibility is critical to being a leader and to being successful.

When writing, be careful of subconscious negatives. These tend to go hand in hand with using unnecessary words and phrases. Too often people put words, phrases, and sentences in their writing that actually negate what they are trying to achieve with their communication.

For example, after finishing a manuscript, aspiring novelists have to write query/cover letters, which is like a résumé for the book and the writer. These are sent to agents and editors, as authors begin the long road toward trying to get published. When I teach, I spend a lot of time on the cover letter, pointing out common mistakes. One is subconscious negatives—words or sentences that reflect negatively on the writer or the book. Starting a query letter with the phrase "I hope you like the book," for example, is a subconscious negative. It indicates fear and uncertainty, because you're telling the person you don't have confidence in what you've done.

Often, query letters bad-mouth the very business the writer is trying to get into, by making comments about how difficult it is to get published and the lack of acumen among agents and editors who fail to see the author's brilliance.

> "The great enemy of clear language is insincerity. When there is a gap between one's real and one's declared aims, one turns as it were instinctively to long words and exhausted idioms, like a cuttlefish squirting out ink."
>
> —GEORGE ORWELL

Exercise 32: COMMUNICATION

You have been doing written communication exercises throughout this book, getting thoughts out of your head and into the real world. Look back at the exercises you've done so far and see how many times you qualified your answers or put subconscious negatives in your writing.

Find two and rewrite them, removing the qualifiers.

STANDING OPERATING PROCEDURES CODIFY AND HELP CHANGE HABITS

Standing operating procedures (SOPs) are anything written down that delineates how things should be done. They can serve many purposes, which we will cover shortly. The key part of the first sentence of this paragraph is *written down*. Once more: Writing something down makes it real. It also makes it easily available. It reduces confusion and misunderstanding.

Every job I've ever done, I've ended up writing an SOP for it. Usually I do this because, surprisingly to me, no one before me did it, even when it was part of their job. I also did it so I could better understand what I was supposed to be doing.

When I finished my Special Forces training at Fort Bragg, I was issued orders assigning me to the 10th Special Forces Group (Airborne) at Fort Devens, Massachusetts. I was assigned to be a team's executive officer. After the team leader had in-briefed me, he asked me if I had any questions. The first thing I did was ask him for the team's SOP, as I had been taught to do at Fort Bragg. I was surprised when he told me they didn't have one. He had explanations why they didn't need one, but ultimately, in retrospect, the primary reason was that no one had taken the initiative to write one, because writing an SOP is a very time-consuming process. It's a "front end–back end" deal. You put the work in on the front end to save you considerably more time in the long run on the back end. Unfortunately, too often, people are overwhelmed up front and don't see the larger, long-range picture.

When I took command of my own A-Team a few months later, once again, the first thing I asked was where the team SOP was. I had been taught at Fort Bragg in the Qualification Course that every team should have an SOP. After my previous experience, I wasn't too surprised when I was told the team didn't have one written down. They "knew" what they needed to do, I was told. Right. And even if *they* did, how was *I* supposed to "know" it?

So I began writing the team SOP. Basically, I began formalizing what everyone said they "knew." I not only drew from my team members' expertise, I went to other teams and found those who did have SOPs and got copies. I went to the company head-quarters and talked to the sergeant major, who had extensive combat experience, and got him to help, giving us some tips—seemingly small, but ones that could save your life in combat.

The team SOP when completed was rather detailed and a living document that we constantly refined as we tested concepts in it and learned what worked and what didn't. The beginning of it was my and my team sergeant's policy letters, spelling out our philosophy for leading the team.

My team sergeant was direct and to the point. Here were some of his choicer lines:

Nothing is impossible to the man who doesn't have to do it.
Smith & Wesson beats four aces.
The latest information hasn't been put out yet.
There are two types of soldiers—the steely-eyed killer and the
   beady-eyed minion.

Here are some excerpts from mine:

The most basic tenet of teamwork is honesty.
With rank and privilege comes responsibility.
Everyone is a leader.
We do everything together.
If you have a problem with someone with higher rank, let me
   know.
Keep a positive attitude.
Discipline stays at the team level.
Be on time.
Keep your sense of humor. You'll need it.

After the policy letters, we then specified who on the team was responsible for what. We took much of this from the field manual for Special Forces that had this information. Again, as mentioned earlier, you can help yourself tremendously when writing an SOP for yourself if you check out what is already out there. Someone, somewhere, probably wrote one just like the one you want to write. Also, your SOP, like your goals, should be in alignment with higher-level SOPs.

We then covered numerous tactical situations and codified how each team member would act. Then we would train on those SOPs until the actions became instinctual.

SOPs codify and set standards

When I was first published I attended a continuing education class on magazine writing. I didn't have plans to write articles, but I figured it was a form of writing, so I would learn something. I was trying to get out of my tunnel vision. The instructor gave out a thin comb-bound booklet covering the material he was going to teach. I thought this was a good idea, and when I was getting ready to teach my first writing class, I did the same.

My first draft of what I called my *Fiction Writer's Toolkit: A Guide to Writing Novels and Getting Published* was eleven pages long. That's how much I *consciously* knew about the subject matter, even though I'd already had three books published. As the years progressed and I wrote more books and taught more, I would continually update the *Toolkit*. After eight years it became over ninety thousand words long and was eventually published by Writer's Digest as *The Novel Writer's Toolkit: A Guide to Writing Great Fiction and Getting It Published*. Does that mean I learned so much new stuff over the years? Yes, but what I also did was begin to move things I "knew" from my subconscious to my conscious. There was no way I would have published three books if all I knew was eleven pages' worth of material about writing books. An SOP is an excellent way to formalize things you already "know" but aren't quite sure that you know.

This book you are reading began in the same way, as I began to write down what we had done in Special Forces, to codify it in a usable format.

Special Operations has always relied on SOPs. If you get a copy of the current U.S. Army Ranger Handbook, which every good infantry and Special Forces officer should be packing, in the very beginning is a list of Rogers' Rules of Ranging. The first Rangers were formed in 1756, and Rogers wrote his rules in 1759 after three years of combat experience on the frontier. Some of these sound quite simple, but they were learned, as many of the lessons in this book were, at the cost of blood:

Don't forget nothing.

Tell the truth about what you see and do.

When you're on the march, act the way you would if you were sneaking up on a deer. See the enemy first.

Don't never take a chance you don't have to.

When we camp, half the party stays awake while the other half sleeps.

Don't ever march home the same way. Take a different route so you won't be ambushed.

And so on—all very basic, but rules that are constantly violated every day by military forces. At the cost of blood.

Whatever your job is, you should have an SOP for it. And it should be written so that someone with no background can achieve a basic level of functioning in the job for a short period of time. Other SOPs should lay out the way your organization works—the way things really work, not how you want someone to think they work.

SOPs are a great way to codify habits you want to develop and also list habits you want to avoid. Writing them down and posting them someplace where you can often see them helps keep you in the real world. As you know from having gotten this far in the book, you won't be able to keep all you've learned or need to do in your head. That's why the exercises require you to write things down—to make them more real for you.

Failure to follow SOPs lays the groundwork for disaster, as is failing to study history. You will see this shortly in the Blood Lesson of The Woman Who Was.

SOPs should be followed, but they should also be evaluated in the face of changing circumstances. SOPs are not written in stone. They need to be checked every once in a while to make sure that they are still applicable and that they are being followed. Having a nice-looking binder with wonderfully written SOPs does you no good if you don't read them or follow them. And SOPs that are out of date can cause more harm than good. They should be constantly updated based on After Action Reviews, which we will cover shortly.

An example of a standing operating procedure I use is a list of my blind spots—those things I have a tendency to do that have a negative effect. I use that list to remind me of character flaws I'm trying to overcome. This list often stops me from screwing up. Another SOP I use is for my physical fitness routine. I list what

I'm doing on each day of the week (bike, run, kayak on certain days) so I have a consistent program. Many of the exercises you've done in this book have given you answers that you can post and use as personal SOPs.

Exercise 33: COMMUNICATION

Pick an aspect of your life (job, hobby, physical fitness program, etc.) and begin to write the SOP for it. Start with the goal (*What*) you laid out for this way back in Exercise 4.

ORAL COMMUNICATION

Oral communication is faster than written. And in the speed of your response lies the danger. Many times, oral communication is action taken in response to something.

You must be careful whenever you react. You must be careful not to speak—to act—without thinking.

Many of the things we discussed under written communication apply to oral communication. Oral communication, however, is more situational. A large part of it depends on whom you are speaking to. A successful person considers his audience's point of view and directs the conversation accordingly, without losing his own point of view.

For example, during the first day of West Point Beast Barracks, called R-Day, for Reception Day, new cadets are run through a meat grinder of checkpoints and instant discipline. A checklist is pinned to the new cadet's uniform with all the places they have to visit that day for in-processing. They are instructed to report to the "man in the red sash," an upperclassman who checks the list and directs cadets onward. Of course, it's not as easy as it sounds.

When you first report to the man in the red sash, you are carrying your bags from home. The man orders you to drop the bags. Most cadets, being normal people, will lower the bags to the ground. The man then orders them to pick the bags back up, and then once more orders them to drop the bags, his voice going up an octave. This process continues until the bewildered new cadets realize they are supposed to drop the bags instantly upon receiving the order. It is the beginning of teaching cadets to instantly and literally obey orders without question.

Since you're not in Beast Barracks, don't be afraid to ask questions or express uncertainty when listening to others speak. If others aren't getting their message across to you, the misunderstanding is not necessarily your fault. Lord Cardigan should have taken a second or two to ask the courier exactly what the objective was, rather than accepting a vague gesture from the courier.

This is particularly crucial in phone conversations, where you aren't given many nonverbal cues. The phone is a necessary tool of our society and one over which much business and personal communication is conducted. For your business, it pays to keep a log of all phone conversations, just like you keep a log of all written messages that come through the mail or via the Internet. In oral communication, ask and answer as many questions as are necessary, to make sure you and the person you're speaking with are on the same page—*before* action is taken.

When communicating through the spoken word, evaluate who you are talking to and adjust accordingly. We've covered differing points of view several times already. In addition to that, you need to gauge the intellectual and experience level of the people you're speaking with, to ensure that they can understand what you're saying.

The actual words that are said, both spoken and written, reveal a great deal about people. If you listen and observe carefully, you can often uncover true motivation. Conflict and disagreement can escalate quickly when a few seemingly innocent words are used.

Be careful when you use slang or abbreviations. Slang often reflects negatively on the speaker. If you use abbreviations, make sure people know what they mean. Too often people assume that the other person understands them, and sometimes the other person isn't willing to admit ignorance. Using abbreviations can also give listeners the impression that you're trying to distance yourself from them or intellectually elevate yourself above them. It pays to be slow and patient and explain things as you need to.

An incident occurred when I was attending the Infantry Officer Advanced Course at Fort Benning, Georgia, that will help illustrate this point. I was older and had more time in grade than most of my classmates. And I had more experience because I had not only done a tour of duty in the infantry, but also gone through Special Forces training and a tour of duty in Special Forces.

We had foreign students going through the course with us. One time I was detailed to brief an operations order I had written. My Special Forces training came through, because instead of the rote recitation the other students were doing, I took my time and slowly went through the order, making sure I explained everything in detail and making sure everyone I was talking to, including the foreign students, clearly understood the order.

The instructor wanted to flunk me. He told me that order

wouldn't have cut it in the 82nd Airborne. In his opinion, I'd explained too much and gone too slowly.

The interesting thing was that every foreign officer came up to me afterward and said that was the first operations order that they had understood since starting the course. Even a few of the American officers said it was the clearest order they'd ever heard.

Too often people get caught up in format, not content. A format is nothing more than a tool to follow. Use it if it works. But if it doesn't work, improvise.

Successful people make sure the content of what they are trying to communicate gets across, regardless of format.

COMMUNICATE: THE ARTIST'S IMAGINATION

As a teacher I've worked with thousands of aspiring writers. As I've said, the percentage who actually were open to learning and improving their craft was around the infamous five-percent mark. The key to success for those few was that they got out of their own point of view and considered the reader. They understood that writing a novel is about entertaining and informing the reader, not about the author's own validation.

I've given many talks to a variety of audiences, and have listened to many speeches. Often, I'll hear speakers tell the story of their life. While this can often be inspiring, rarely do such stories give practical information that the listeners can take away with them and use.

To be a successful communicator, you have to make sure that what you're saying is about the people receiving the communication, not about you—the person sending it.

TAKE *COMMAND* OF YOUR CHANGE

INTRODUCTION

"We are all warriors in the battle of life, but some lead and others follow."

—KAHLIL GIBRAN

A successful person must be a leader first:

- You must be able to lead yourself.
- You must be able to interact with others and lead them.

You can't count on others to bring you to a successful level in life.

Others can help. But the only person you can count on one hundred percent of the time is yourself. Because of this, you must develop and master personal leadership.

To be different from the majority, to be successful, you must find your way out of the pack and along a difficult road. If you don't exercise personal leadership, you will be under the control of those around you, whose goals might not be in line with your own goals.

No one else can hand you what you want to achieve—you have to earn it.

SPECIAL FORCES ASSESSMENT AND SELECTION THOUGHT:
Challenges can be stepping stones or stumbling blocks.
It's all in your perspective.

BLOOD LESSON: THE WOMAN WHO WAS

"In wartime, truth is so precious that she should always be
attended by a bodyguard of lies."

—WINSTON CHURCHILL

We've examined the story of the Man Who Never Was—an example of goal setting and one-sentence problem solving. This Blood Lesson is about a very brave woman who, most tragically, did exist.

The first covert female radio operator sent into occupied France was Noor Inayat Khan. While she displayed extraordinary bravery and paid the ultimate price, she failed to exercise the personal leadership required to assess her situation—a failure that cost others their lives as well.

The problem

As World War II raged on, a resistance movement began to flourish in the occupied countries. To assist these movements, the British Special Operations Executive (SOE) parachuted in units called Jedburgh Teams to assist the Resistance (these were the forerunners of Special Forces). In the fog of war, spy-versus-spy betrayal was a constant factor. Despite having the best intentions, an operative needed to exercise personal leadership to evaluate every situation and prevent disaster.

Khan came from an Indian Muslim family—her elder brother

eventually became the head of the Sufi Order International. She was living with her family in Paris when the Germans invaded. They fled to England. Khan joined the Women's Auxiliary Air Force and was trained as a wireless (radio) operator. Because of her fluency in French and her wireless skills, she was recruited by the SOE as an operative.

Some of her trainers felt she was an unsuitable candidate for covert work, because her ethnic background and beauty caused her to stand out in a crowd. Nevertheless, on the night of June 16, 1943, she was flown into France and joined a Resistance network.

Within a month and a half the network was rolled up by the Gestapo. There is some speculation that the British knew the network had already been compromised and sent Khan in, expecting her to be captured and give up information—false information—she had been fed in training: a living version of the Man Who Never Was. Some say she was betrayed by another female agent out of jealousy because Khan had become the lover of that woman's ex.

The solution

Although Khan was brave and did not speak under interrogation, she'd been overly conscientious in her job and had violated Standing Operating Procedures—she'd kept copies of all her messages. The Germans, therefore, were able to begin transmitting, imitating her.

Her handlers in London allegedly failed to note anomalies in "her" transmissions. They dropped three more agents into France because of one of these transmissions, and the Gestapo arrested the agents at the drop zone. Again, there is speculation the handlers knew exactly what they were doing—executing a version of the Man Who Never Was, but with live bodies this time.

Khan—and one of the agents captured because of her messages—were taken to Dachau and executed on September 12, 1944.

The lesson

As you learned under *Character*, any trait taken to an extreme is dangerous. Khan took her passion for her duty to an extreme that backfired. Certainly, her courage cannot be questioned. But her command of herself and the situation wasn't solid.

She failed to do something all Special Forces soldiers are taught: to take command of the situation and question her orders and her assignment. We're taught to always consider the possibility that our orders aren't exactly what they appear to be. We learn to make our own plan, in case everything goes wrong—catastrophe planning, as already described in this book. Responsibility is one of the trademarks of Special Forces leadership.

No matter what happens around you, you ultimately retain full responsibility for your own actions.

Noor Inayat Khan was posthumously awarded a George Cross, Britain's highest award for gallantry not on the battlefield. The citation reads:

"The King has been graciously pleased to approve the posthumous award of the George Cross to Assistant Section Officer Nora Inayat Khan (9901), Women's Auxiliary Air Force. Assistant Section Officer Nora Inayat Khan was the first woman operator to be infiltrated into enemy-occupied France, and was landed by Lysander aircraft on 16th June, 1943. During the weeks immediately following her arrival, the

Gestapo made mass arrests in the Paris Resistance groups to which she had been detailed. She refused however to abandon what had become the principal and most dangerous post in France, although given the opportunity to return to England, because she did not wish to leave her French comrades without communications and she hoped also to rebuild her group. She remained at her post therefore and did the excellent work which earned her a posthumous Mention in Despatches.

"The Gestapo had a full description of her, but knew only her code name 'Madeleine.' They deployed considerable forces in their effort to catch her and so break the last remaining link with London. After three months she was betrayed to the Gestapo and taken to their H.Q. in the Avenue Foch. The Gestapo had found her codes and messages and were now in a position to work back to London. They asked her to co-operate, but she refused and gave them no information of any kind. She was imprisoned in one of the cells on the fifth floor of the Gestapo H.Q. and remained there for several weeks during which time she made two unsuccessful attempts at escape. She was asked to sign a declaration that she would make no further attempts but she refused and the Chief of the Gestapo obtained permission from Berlin to send her to Germany for 'safe custody.' She was the first agent to be sent to Germany.

"Assistant Section Officer Inayat Khan was sent to Karlsruhe in November, 1943, and then to Pforsheim where her cell was apart from the main prison. She was considered to be a particularly dangerous and unco-operative prisoner. The Director of the prison has also been interrogated and has confirmed that Assistant Section Officer Inayat Khan, when interrogated by the Karlsruhe Gestapo, refused to give any information whatsoever, either as to her work or her colleagues.

"She was taken with three others to Dachau Camp on the 12th

September, 1944. On arrival, she was shot and taken to the cre-matorium.

"Assistant Section Officer Inayat Khan displayed the most con-spicuous courage, both moral and physical, over a period of more than 12 months."

THE PURPOSE OF LEADERSHIP

A leader is a person who makes decisions and then implements a course of action. Since a successful person is someone who takes action, that person is, by definition, a leader.

The first thing a leader must do is set goals. Then the leader must make a decision, leading to a course of action that implements sustained change. Ultimately, a leader must take care of himself or herself, and then take care of others.

The first person you must understand how to lead is yourself. That's why I spent so much time in Area Two: Who on character. You need to figure out your personality type and your blind spot. Successful people overcome their weaknesses, and the first step in doing that is identifying the weaknesses. This skill immediately separates those who want to be successful from the majority of the bell curve.

When I teach leadership, I focus first on getting leaders to look at themselves and their personal leadership before looking at their leadership of others.

SPECIAL OPERATIONS LEADERSHIP

I believe the type of leadership we utilize in Special Operations is ideally suited to develop successful individual leadership. Units in

Special Operations are small, and the soldiers well trained and internally motivated. Their missions are usually above the military norm. Special Forces often operates far removed from the normal military chain of command.

There are two key elements of Special Operations leadership:

- Honesty
- Integrity

HONESTY

Honesty is the foundation of respect. Without honesty, all other aspects of what you learn in *Who Dares Wins* fall apart. Special Operations Forces, which conduct covert and secret operations, rely on honesty a great deal. You may find that curious. But it is the very nature of their missions that requires a higher degree of internal honesty from SOF members and teams.

Honesty is your key to dealing with those around you. You cannot expect people to be honest with you if you aren't honest with them. And first and foremost, you need to be honest with yourself.

We all have secrets, and those secrets are often rooted in our deepest fears. Bringing your secrets into the light of day seems daunting. But in reality, once you've achieved this step, the result is rarely ever as bad as you expected it to be. Most people care more about themselves than they do about you. Many people overestimate how others are going to react to their secrets.

Exercise 34: COMMAND

Write down a truth about yourself that you've never told anyone.

Now write down why you haven't told anyone. What are you afraid would happen if you did? How does that fear hold you back?

This fear is subconsciously debilitating to you, especially if it is about something that is ongoing in your life. It most likely means you either need to stop doing whatever it is, or expand this action into your comfort zone so that you can be honest about it.

Your honesty is the touchstone of good communication with those you interact with and those you lead. Remember, we teach people how to treat us.

I spoke with another Special Forces team leader about serving in Afghanistan. He made the point that the Afghanis treated American units differently, depending on how the American units first treated the Afghanis. Those teams that made themselves the honest, but bad-ass, sheriff in town were treated with respect.

Quickly admitting you are wrong—when you are—is a very powerful tool. It disarms those around you. It allows you to focus on fixing a problem rather than defending your position, which is already a bad one, since you're wrong. Admitting when you're wrong builds trust and allows for better communication—especially when you need help.

Exercise 35: COMMAND

Write down something you've done wrong in the past week.

Did you acknowledge the mistake to yourself? To anyone else?

Acknowledge it to someone else (especially the person you did the wrong to) and see what their reaction is.

When you are honest with other people, the threat of the unknown is reduced. The unknown is one of the great causes of fear. If people feel information is being withheld from them, they won't just ignore the feeling, they will start coming up with their own answers. Most of the time their imagination will come up with something far worse than the reality. Being honest induces trust and reduces fear, both within yourself and with others.

INTEGRITY

The word *integrity* comes from the Latin word *integritas*, which means "wholeness," "completeness," and "entirety."

A Roman soldier, when being inspected by his centurion, would strike his fist on the armor over his heart and shout, *"Integritas."* The armor was thicker there than anywhere else. In the same manner, your armor must be strongest around the most vulnerable parts of your successful character. Focusing on and building integrity is the best way to make sure that happens.

Integrity is the opposite of the emotional defenses around our defects. Integrity is the emotional shield around the part of us that is daring and willing to take risks.

People without integrity ignore their blind spots. And they hide other aspects of their character—often from themselves—because they are afraid. You must strive for completeness of character.

Completeness means all parts of your character are oriented toward the same goal rather than conflicting with one another. As you've learned, most people are the causes of their own failure. Accordingly, you can also be the cause of your success.

Integrity is outward-oriented, and requires that you understand the environment in which you live, and respect and understand those with whom you interact. It requires you to make your place in the world, and to make that place count—for your own good as well as others'.

Command of self is taking action in the face of fear.

Facing and dealing with fear is at the core of your ability to move from being ordinary to being successful. How you deal with fear is also about how you apply honesty and integrity in your life, your actions, and your decision making. Understanding your character and that of others is certainly important. And setting goals gives you direction.

The Circle of Success tools won't change anything by themselves, though. Not until your personal command begins to break you from the chains of fear.

COMMAND OF SELF: THE ARTIST'S IMAGINATION

As an author it took me a long time to accept the reality of publishing: I control the quality of the books I write. I don't control the actions of my editor, my publisher, the bookstore, etc. Trying to control those things is a waste of time and energy, and very emotionally draining. I learned to put that energy into the thing I do control—my writing—and to take command of that.

For a long time, I expected my agent to come up with a career plan for me. It took me years before I realized that my agents could never have done this. Each of them helped me, but I had to take command of—exercise personal leadership over—my career, and then ask for their help. I had to make the plan. I had to set the goals. And I had to take responsibility.

COMPLETE THE CIRCLE OF SUCCESS AND CHANGE

INTRODUCTION

You've reached the last tool. Is it clearer now why I call the nine tools of *Who Dares Wins* the Circle of Success? Each of the Special Forces tools you've learned can be used alone, but true success comes when you integrate all the tools. You will continue to refine the exercises in this book as you go forward into your life.

That's why I positioned *Command* at Tool Eight—because it is when you exercise personal leadership that you begin to pull all the tools together.

It is now time to complete the Circle of Success.

SPECIAL FORCES ASSESSMENT AND SELECTION THOUGHT:
You don't get to be number one by aspiring to be number two.

BLOOD LESSON: THE GREEN BERET WAY

Every tool in this book is used to train Green Berets in the Special Forces Qualification Course (Q-Course).

The problem

Special Forces was founded in 1952 by veterans of the Office of Strategic Services, like Colonel Volckman. These officers designed the course using the blood lessons they'd learned in World War II.

The core concept of Special Forces has remained the same for over half a century, even as warfare and technology have evolved and the threats facing our country have changed. The Q-Course has had to evolve, of course, and I was part of a committee that met at Fort Bragg in the mid-eighties to modernize the Q-Course.

The lesson

Applicants who pass Special Forces Assessment and Selection receive orders to permanently change their duty station to Fort Bragg. Only then do they face the Special Forces Qualification Course.

While evaluating Q-Course students, instructors focus on twelve attributes:

1. Intelligence
2. Stability
3. Physical fitness
4. Judgment
5. Motivation
6. Decisiveness
7. Accountability
8. Influence
9. Trustworthiness
10. Teamwork
11. Maturity
12. Communication

Do these look familiar?

The Q-Course pulls together all the elements of *Who Dares Wins:*

What	The course goal is to train Green Berets.
Why	The intent is to produce the best unconventional warrior on the planet.
Where	Training takes place in several locations, each designed to fit a particular expertise required to be a successful warrior.
Character	Assessment and Selection begins with instructors' character analysis of each student. Every step of Q-Course continues the ongoing evaluation.
Change	Successful candidates graduate the Q-Course as very different people from the ones who entered.
Courage	Training is difficult, with a seventy-percent failure rate. Candidates must dig deep within themselves in order to pass.
Communicate	They will be members of a successful team, and their primary mission will be to teach others. Without successful communication skills, they would fail, so communication is emphasized throughout Q-Course training.
Command	Every graduate is taught to be a leader. Each will become part of an A-Team, where individual and group leadership is essential.
Complete	The final Q-Course exercise—called Robin Sage—is the most challenging. All the skills a candidate has learned must be integrated and used at a successful level.

The solution

On average, only thirty percent of students make it to the point of successfully completing the Robin Sage exercise. That's only thirty percent of the best of the best in the military.

Finally the student is no longer a student. Technically, at least. "Graduates" ship out to various Special Forces field groups and are assigned to A-Teams—where they quickly find out they have a lot to learn. Thus, the practical experience of operating on a real A-Team begins. So, just like you, they continue on their Circle of

Success journey, constantly learning and improving for the rest of their lives.

The lesson

The Q-Course continues to evolve and change, as more blood lessons are learned on battlefields all over the world. And you need to continue to evolve and change as you work your *Who Dares Wins* program—as you rework and refine the Circle again and again on your own battlefields of life. What you have as you complete this book is a framework for a plan of action for change. A beginning. Never stop learning.

Here, again, is the Circle of Success:

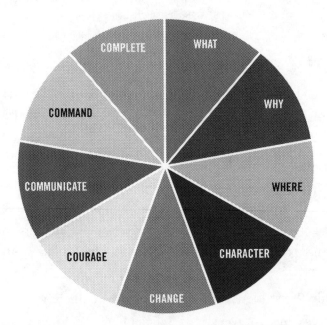

Envision yourself standing at the center of the circle. All the tools converge at the center—you. They're all connected. You've worked with all of them and have completed many exercises.

The Circle is not a one-time thing. Each pass from Tool Nine back to Tool One peels away another layer, circling closer and closer to uncovering the "true" you that you desire to be.

Now it's time to come up with one more plan.

Exercise 36: COMPLETE

Pick a goal from your list in Exercise 1 that you've yet to work with, perhaps one that has changed, that you've refined, as you've worked through the later tools.

Take the rest of the tools in order and write a short summary of what needs to happen under each tool, just like I did in the blood lesson for the Q-Course.

This is your chance to pull together everything you've learned about how to become successful in your life. Review each tool as needed.

AFTER ACTION REVIEWS

Once you've implemented your plan, it's time to use another Special Forces tool—the After Action Review (AAR). This is used by Special Forces to objectively determine if a mission's goal has been achieved. In fact, whenever you think you have finished doing something significant, you should conduct an AAR.

A person who won't look closely at him- or herself is someone who is doomed to keep doing the same things wrong again and again.

Because simulated combat exercises are so difficult to observe and judge, the military designed the AAR to help the participants figure out what happened. It was only in the late 1990s that the business world began picking up the concept, most likely as a result of military officers filtering into the civilian world and bringing what they had learned with them. A Harvard Business School professor wrote an article about it in the *Harvard Business Review* in 1993, which I suppose made it more highbrow than a squad of grunts sitting around trying to figure out what just happened. The most critical aspect of having an effective AAR is honesty. The first, and most important, question to be answered is, "Was the goal or mission accomplished?" Given that your goal or mission was originally stated clearly in one sentence, the answer should be clear.

I have read several business books that say an AAR should not judge success or failure. I disagree with that. The theory is that focusing on success or failure will cause emotional conflict. If that's the case, then so be it. We succeed. We fail. We learn, adjust, and move on. Successful people have to break through the conflict that comes with not succeeding all the time.

Remember the stages of change: denial, anger, bargaining, depression, acceptance. If failure at a goal is a conflict for you, it's one of your blind spots. Work through these changes until you've conquered the associated fear.

If the answer is yes, you achieved your goal, then pat yourself on the back and see what fine-tuning needs to be done. If the answer is no, hunker down until the smoke clears—until you have solid answers from your AAR and know what changes need to be made to your plan.

STEPS FOR AN EFFECTIVE AAR

1. Did you achieve your goal?
2. Review your plan. Did you follow your plan? If not, note the exceptions and variations you made. Did the rule breaking of the plan work? If it didn't, take responsibility.

3. Review the preparation for the activity. This means go over all the tools listed in this book, and determine if each tool was effectively applied to your plan. If not, note areas of improvement or refinement you could have made.

4. Summarize the events as they occurred, using a detailed timeline, with no commentary—just the facts. Build a complete timeline of action.

5. Focus on why each specific action was taken, and note whether each step of the plan was followed or deviated from (which is not necessarily a bad thing). Give particular focus to when fear played a role in your actions—this is the most difficult part of the AAR, but the most critical. Fear is most likely where your actions diverged from your plan.

6. Examine what role SOPs played. Did they work? Do they need to be revised?

7. Summarize areas of plan improvement and refinement, as well as alternative actions you could have taken to achieve a more successful result.

Exercise 37: COMPLETE

Conduct an After Action Review for your plan from Exercise 36. With your AAR done, incorporate all you've learned into a modified plan, then do it over again. Repeat as necessary until it achieves the change and goal you desire.

RULE BREAKING

Successful people must have a sense of confidence that enables them to break the rules when needed. But they must also have a clearly defined reason for breaking a rule.

There are three *rules* for rule breaking:

1. *Know the rule.*
Breaking a rule because you're ignorant of it is simply being, well, ignorant.
2. *Have a good reason for breaking the rule.*
You know the rule. Objectively study how it factors into achieving plan success, and break it only if you think doing so will bring you greater success.
3. *Take responsibility for breaking the rule.*
If breaking the rule works out, great. If it doesn't, it's on you. Own the result, either way. That's integrity—a cornerstone of a successful person's character.

To succeed in life and break out of the ordinary, you are going to have to break some rules.

COMPLETE: THE ARTIST'S IMAGINATION

The components of a successful novel can be broken down into Circle of Success tools:

- WHAT: The idea and plot.
- WHY: Intent.
- WHERE: Setting.
- CHARACTER: The key element in the story; you must understand yours as a writer.
- CHANGE: Character arc, and learning to be a better writer.
- COURAGE: You have to dare to be different.

- COMMUNICATE: The writing itself.
- COMMAND: As the author, you are responsible for the book.
- COMPLETE: You have to finish the book.

Like the tools you've learned in *Who Dares Wins*, each story component by itself does not make a novel. A writer must pull all the aspects of his story together into one coherent whole before the reader will follow him and his characters on the journey (the mission) he's created.

For most writers, trying to define the entirety of a novel before doing the first bit of planning is an overwhelming task. It's often much more effective and less intimidating for the writer to develop a story piece by piece, building the whole out of the parts.

Who Dares Wins is your opportunity to focus on piece-by-piece development, as you build toward your successful whole. Work on each tool, one at a time. And gradually, you will learn how to put the pieces together and win.

Looking at it another way, consider *Who Dares Wins* a life plan.

It takes continuous work on every *Who Dares Wins* tool, and a lifetime commitment to continue following the Circle of Success—pulling each tool closer to the next until they intertwine—to create an integrated, successful person.

DARES, THE GREEN BERET WAY

INTRODUCTION

You've learned everything you need to know about the Circle of Success. You have the tools you need to *Conquer Fear and Succeed*.

Now the choice lies with you. You must determine the path your life takes.

ONE FINAL BLOOD LESSON: ROBIN SAGE

The culminating exercise of the Special Forces Qualification Course is called Robin Sage. Robin Sage is designed to be as realistic a mission simulation as can be accomplished in a training environment.

The problem

Robin Sage is the fourth phase of the Q-Course. After being transported to Camp Mackall, the students are broken down into A-Teams and required to put their successful knowledge and skills to use in a nineteen-day problem-solving Field Training Exercise (and yes, this is a blood lesson, as men have died during this exercise).

Robin Sage is an unconventional warfare exercise in which students must deal not only with other students, but also with counterinsurgent and guerrilla personnel, auxiliary personnel, and instructors. Realism is stressed above all else.

The student teams must train a mock guerrilla force in a hostile environment, using civilians in the surrounding community as their auxiliary manpower. This exercise ranges over approximately fifty thousand square miles of North Carolina countryside. By the conclusion of Robin Sage, the students have been placed in many stressful situations in which they are required to use their individual skills, their leadership skills, and their ability to work in adverse and ambiguous conditions.

One thing to remember about the lengths of these various courses and exercises: Don't think of each day in the civilian terms of an eight- to ten-hour workday, and then home for a beer. The nineteen days of Robin Sage is a grueling, often spirit-breaking, 24/7 experience.

The solution

The evaluation of a Special Forces student in Robin Sage is about much more than whether he completed his mission. It's about being the best soldier he can be and operating on a team. Students are graded not only on how well they accomplish their individual tasks, but also on how well their team does.

They are graded on all aspects of *Who Dares Wins*, not just a particular specialty.

You might consider your life to be Robin Sage, a constant testing environment in which you can get better and more confident with each new experience.

KNOWLEDGE IS USELESS IF NOT USED

If you've read this book up to this point, it was most likely the equivalent of trying to take a sip of water from a fire hydrant. A lot came at you. Some of it seemed very simple and basic to you, and some of it you probably still don't "get" yet. Even some of the simple stuff may have appeared easy, but once you tried doing it, you found just how deceiving appearances can be.

Do you want to be successful?

I asked this question at the beginning of the book. Now that you are at the end, you have a better idea of what taking a successful life path will require—what it will mean to succeed in the face of fear.

Now you need to ask yourself the same question, and you need to answer it again honestly. A half effort won't get you where you want to be. A ninety-five-percent effort will not succeed. You must be totally committed to the choice you've made— to the Circle of Success.

Exercise 38: YOUR MOMENTS OF ENLIGHTENMENT

Time to pull it all together. Fold a piece of paper in thirds. Label the left column MOE. In it, write down the answers to these questions—make them real.

While drinking from the hydrant that is this book:

- What stood out?
- What angered you?

- What made you afraid?
- What motivated you?
- What excited you?
- What did you think was dumb?
- What did you think was smart?
- What did you think wouldn't work?
- What did you think was something you could use right away?
- What did you want to know more about?

Your answers to these questions are new moments of enlightenment for you to analyze and build future decisions and actions from, using everything you've learned.

Exercise 39: YOUR DECISIONS

Using the paper from Exercise 38, label the center column *Decisions*, and write down what decision you want to make regarding your moments of enlightenment.

Exercise 40: YOUR SUSTAINED ACTION

Using the paper from Exercise 39, label the right column *Sustained Actions*, and write down what sustained action you will have to do in order to change.

As you've learned, the Circle of Success is an ongoing cycle of change—one moment of enlightenment leads to another, and then another. If reading and working through the *Who Dares Wins* tools has helped you rise out of the mundane and fear-filled, it's not time to kick back, light a cigar, and think you've made it.

To continue to improve, you must work through the Circle again. All the *Who Dares Wins* exercises are listed once more in Appendix B. Do them again. All of them. And then do them again.

With each new pass, compare the new answers you write down to the ones you've written previously. You should see your point of view changing each time. Your new reality compared to your world before.

INTEGRATION AND TIGHTNESS

Who Dares Wins is made up of many pieces and parts: three major areas, with three tools each, that make up the Circle of Success. Tightness of effort and integrity is a sign of the successful. I've made numerous cross-references throughout this book, indicating where one subject touched on another. Those cross-references show you the tightness you need to achieve in your efforts, the way one part of the circle depends on another.

As you saw in some of the blood lessons, succeeding in several areas of *Who Dares Wins*, but not in all, can lead to disaster. In fact, partial success can be a very dangerous thing. Inayat Khan certainly had tremendous *Courage*, but problems in *Command* and *Communication* cost lives.

It is essential to keep all the parts of *Who Dares Wins* and your Circle of Success tightly integrated.

LIVING A SUCCESSFUL LIFE

Living a successful life—really succeeding—begins and ends with you. Many people fail and succumb to fear as they try to follow a successful path. They expend their energy trying to change the world around them, rather than themselves, and the world resists.

Dare to focus on becoming the person you want to be first. Focus on understanding your own true path. Once you achieve a measure of success in that, only then is it time to move out into the world and dare to focus on how you interact with others and the paths they're taking.

And every step of the way, remember:

WHO DARES WINS.

IMMEDIATE ACTION DRILLS— THE CIRCLE OF SUCCESS PATH

1. *What* **do you want to change and achieve?**

Write down each goal you want to achieve, in one sentence.

Check the verb in each sentence, and make sure it is a positive
verb and is an action you control.

Make sure the outcome of each goal is something that you can
observe, so you will know when you've achieved the goal.

Check your goals for inherent conflict.

2. *Why* **do you want to change and achieve your goals?**

Using your one-sentence goals, write down *Why* you want to
achieve each goal; for example: "I am doing *this* goal for *this*
reason."

Examine your *Why* for options on how you can achieve the goal.

Examine your *Why* to set boundaries for your goal, so you don't
go to extremes.

3. *Where* will change occur?

Examine your environment and see who and what will aid you in achieving your *What* and changing.

Figure out who and what are hindering you from achieving your *What* and changing, and take steps to get rid of those distractions or negate them.

Research your *What* (goals) and *Why* (intent).

4. Understand your *Character*.

Character is your core personality, both positive and negative.

Study your actions to determine your character and true nature.

Work on possessing the character traits of successful people: open-mindedness; willingness to surrender when wrong; balancing desire and contentment; having patience and self-discipline; using an active imagination and setting goals.

Understand that emotion is more powerful than intellect.

Figure out your *Character*, both strengths and weaknesses, by profiling your habits and also by comparing yourself to character templates, such as the Myers-Briggs (pages 82 and 196).

5. What is *Change* and how do you do it?

Understand and implement the three steps of change:

1. Have a moment of enlightenment.
2. Make a decision.
3. Implement sustained action.

6. How do you build the *Courage* to change?

Going back to *Character*, look at the character type that is the opposite of yours in the Myers-Briggs and see what you are afraid of doing, then force yourself to do that.

Find your blind spots by using the traits, needs, flaws paradigm (page 112).

Expand your comfort zone by repeatedly venturing into your courage zone.

Catastrophe plan the various aspects of your life, predicting what the worst-case scenario would be, and then getting ready to face it.

7. *Communicate* your change to the world.

The purpose of communication is to evoke a desired response.

Writing things down makes them real and delineates responsibility.

Read and listen carefully to get the true message being communicated by others.

8. Take *Command* of your change.

You are in *Command* of everything you say and do.

You must have honesty and integrity as part of your personal leadership traits.

9. *Complete* the Circle of Success and change.

Integrate and align the previous eight tools.

Use the three rules of rule-breaking to break out of the mundane and become successful:

1. Know the rule.
2. Have a good reason for breaking the rule.
3. Take responsibility for breaking the rule.

WHO DARES WINS EXERCISES

Exercise 1: TAKE THE CHALLENGE

Record the one thing you fear the most. (The fear in your head is not in the real world. Writing down your fear externalizes it, so you can take action to conquer it in the real world.)

Exercise 2: TAKE THE CHALLENGE

Record the one thing that motivates you the most.

Exercise 3: WHAT

In one sentence, write down a short-term goal that you want to achieve this week.

Exercise 4: WHAT

Divide a piece of lined paper into four equal columns.

Label each column: *What, Why, Where, Done.*

Under the first column, *What,* write a subordinate goal for each of the areas that apply in which you want to achieve a goal in the next week (nothing major, just a basic, simple goal).

The areas can be: Academic, Physical, Family, Relationship, Hobby, Spiritual, Professional, Task, Financial, etc.

Exercise 5: WHY

Using the four-column sheet from Exercise 4, fill out the second column. Next to each *What*, list the *Why* in the second column. I am doing X (*What*) for reason Y (*Why*).

Exercise 6: WHERE

Take a piece of paper. Fold it in thirds. In the left column write down the *What* you listed in column one of Exercise 4.

Label the middle column *My WHERE As It Is Now.*

Label the right column *My WHERE As It Should Be.*

List in the middle column those people and things that currently are part of your *Where* and how they affect it.

List in the right column how you would like your *Where* to be in order for it to be a positive environment.

Exercise 7: WHERE

Using the four-column sheet from Exercise 4, fill out the third column. Next to each *What* and *Why*, list the *Where* as it should be in the third column.

Exercise 8: WINS

Using your four-column sheet from Exercise 4, pick one of the *What*'s. Using the *Why* and *Where* you've already added, apply the CARVER formula to the goal to see if you can achieve it. If you can, then you can check column four—*Done*.

This doesn't mean the *What* is actually done; it means your planning for it is done. You can apply this formula to all your *What*'s.

Exercise 9: CHARACTER

Define yourself in one sentence.

Exercise 10: CHARACTER

On the same sheet as Exercise 9, describe a moment when you were under extreme stress and pressure and had to make a decision. List the cause of the stress and pressure.

Exercise 11: CHARACTER

On the same sheet you used for Exercises 9 and 10, describe your reaction to that moment and the decision you made.

In retrospect, was it a good decision, or could you have chosen better?

Exercise 12: CHARACTER

Describe the last time you were told you were doing something wrong and how you responded to it.

Describe your reaction in terms of the five parts of the Kübler-Ross scale.

Did you make it to acceptance and change?

If not, where did you stop and why?

Exercise 13: CHARACTER

Take a piece of paper. Draw a line down the middle. Label the left side *To Do*. Label the right side *Done*.

List down the left side everything you have to do tomorrow.

Then, when you do one of your *To Do*'s, cross it off and write what you've done on the right side. Thus you can literally see your balance between desire and contentment on one page for one day.

Exercise 14: CHARACTER

Look at your *To Do/Done* list from Exercise 13. Are there some *To Do*'s that aren't really needed, that you've actually had on your *To Do* list a long time and never gotten around to? Maybe you shouldn't do them at all. Close some doors. Get rid of options that distract from your main goals. Are there people in your life you hold on to and expend energy on out of fear?

Exercise 15: CHARACTER

Remember the four-column *What, Why, Where, Done* list you began in
Exercise 4? For every *What* that has not been *Done*, pencil in a deadline
for when it should be done.

    The clock is now ticking.

Exercise 16: CHARACTER

Describe the last time you felt anger or guilt. (If you can't remember, then
notice the *next* time you feel either of those emotions.) Write the event down.
What specifically provoked the emotion? Why did this situation touch your flash
point? Simply understanding this dynamic will make you stronger the next time
your flash point is touched.

Exercise 17: CHARACTER

For the next twenty-four hours, write down everything you do. Simply list every
action without comment. Let the list sit for several days. Then look at the list
with an open mind. Describe what kind of person would do these things.

    Then answer these questions: "Is this the kind of person I want to be? Are
these the things I really want to be spending my time doing?"

Exercise 18: CHARACTER

Pick A or B for each of the four areas that best describe you:

AREA 1

Block A	**Block B**
Act first, think later?	Think first, then act?
Feel deprived if cut off from world?	Need private time to get energized?
Motivated by outside world?	Internally motivated?
Get energized by groups?	Groups drain your energy?

AREA 2

Block A	**Block B**
Mentally live in the now?	Mentally live in the future?
Use common sense for practical solutions?	Use imagination for innovative solutions?
Memory focuses on details and facts?	Memory focuses on patterns and context?
Don't like guessing?	Like guessing?

AREA 3

Block A	**Block B**
Search for facts to make a decision?	Go with feelings to make a decision?
Notice work to be accomplished?	Focus on people's needs?
Tend to provide an objective analysis?	Seek consensus and popular opinion?
Believe conflict is all right?	Dislike conflict and avoid it at all costs?

AREA 4

Block A	**Block B**
Plan detail before taking action?	Are comfortable taking action without a plan?
Complete tasks in order?	Like to multitask?
Stay ahead of deadlines?	Work best close to deadlines?
Set goals, deadlines, and routines?	Like to be flexible and avoid commitments?

THE RESULTS:

1A = Extrovert (E)	1B = Introvert (I)
2A = Sensing (S)	2B = iNtuition (N)
3A = Thinking (T)	3B = Feeling (F)
4A = Judging (J)	4B = Perceiving (P)

List out your four letters. You are one of sixteen Myers-Briggs character types:

INTP = Architect	ESFJ = Seller
ENTP = Inventor	ISFJ = Conservator
INTJ = Scientist	ESFP = Entertainer
ENTJ = Field Marshal	ISFP = Artist
INFP = Questor	ESTJ = Administrator
ENFP = Journalist	ISTJ = Trustee
INFJ = Author	ESTP = Promoter
ENFJ = Pedagogue	ISTP = Artisan

Exercise 19: CHANGE

Fold a piece of paper in thirds. On the left third, write down three moments of enlightenment you've had since beginning this book.

Exercise 20: CHANGE

Using the paper from Exercise 19, in the middle column, write down a decision to change based on each of the three moments of enlightenment.

Exercise 21: CHANGE

For each decision to change you listed in Exercise 20, in the right column, define the sustained action you would have to do to achieve the change you desire.

Exercise 22: CHANGE

Using your goal-aligned training program from Exercises 19–21, list the standards you need to meet to achieve sustained change. Post these standards where you can see them every day. Make the standards external goals that can clearly be assessed—you either achieve the standard or you don't.

Exercise 23: COURAGE

In one word, record what you believe to be your greatest character trait.

Exercise 24: COURAGE

Using that trait, write down the corresponding need and potential flaw (blind spot).

Exercise 25: COURAGE

Describe the last time you wanted to do something you knew was the right thing to do, but you didn't do it. What kept you from doing it?

Exercise 26: COURAGE

Based on what you've uncovered in this Tool and under *Character*, list those traits, needs, and flaws that you feel compromise your character. Then list the fears (blind spots) that you suspect hurt you.

Exercise 27: COURAGE

Think back to the last really bad thing that happened to you. Write it down. Then write down the warning signs that were present before it happened, but that you didn't focus on.

These warning signs are fear indicators that you should write down and post so that you can see them every day. Read them, focus on them, and determine if they are coming up again with regard to something else in your life.

Exercise 28: COURAGE

Based on your answer to Exercise 26, pick one flaw and write down one positive act that would challenge you to face that blind spot, act in the face of fear, and enter your courage zone.

Exercise 29: COURAGE

For the next week, do this one positive act every day. By the end of the week, your comfort zone will have expanded.

Exercise 30: COURAGE

Fold a piece of paper in half, and on the left side, for the following areas, write down a potential catastrophe that could occur:

Physical

Financial

Natural disaster

Work

Relationship

The next major task you have to do

Exercise 31: COURAGE

On the right side of the paper from Exercise 30, write out your plan in case the catastrophe occurs and make the necessary preparations.

Exercise 32: COMMUNICATION

You have been doing written communication exercises throughout this book, getting thoughts out of your head and into the real world. Look back at the exercises you've done so far and see how many times you qualified your answers or put subconscious negatives in your writing.

Find two and rewrite them, removing the qualifiers.

Exercise 33: COMMUNICATION

Pick an aspect of your life (job, hobby, physical fitness program, etc.) and begin to write the standing operating procedure for it. Start with the goal (*What*) you laid out for this way back in Exercise 4.

Exercise 34: COMMAND

Write down a truth about yourself that you've never told anyone.

Now write down why you haven't told anyone. What are you afraid would happen if you did? How does that fear hold you back?

This fear is subconsciously debilitating to you, especially if it is about something that is ongoing in your life. It most likely means you either need to stop doing whatever it is, or expand this action into your comfort zone so that you can be honest about it.

Exercise 35: COMMAND

Write down something you've done wrong in the past week.

Did you acknowledge the mistake to yourself? To anyone else?

Acknowledge it to someone else (especially the person you did the wrong to) and see what their reaction is.

Exercise 36: COMPLETE

Pick a goal from your list in Exercise 1 that you've yet to work with, perhaps one that has changed, that you've refined, as you've worked through the later tools.

Take the rest of the tools in order and write a short summary of what needs to happen under each tool, just like I did in the blood lesson for the Q-Course.

This is your chance to pull together everything you've learned about how to become successful in your life. Review each tool as needed.

Exercise 37: COMPLETE

Conduct an After Action Review for your plan from Exercise 36. With your AAR done, incorporate all you've learned into a modified plan, then do it over again. Repeat as necessary until it achieves the change and goal you desire.

Exercise 38: YOUR MOMENTS OF ENLIGHTENMENT

Time to pull it all together. Fold a piece of paper in thirds. Label the left column MOE. In it, write down the answers to these questions—make them real.

While drinking from the hydrant that is this book:

- What stood out?
- What angered you?
- What made you afraid?
- What motivated you?
- What excited you?
- What did you think was dumb?
- What did you think was smart?
- What did you think wouldn't work?
- What did you think was something you could use right away?
- What did you want to know more about?

Your answers to these questions are new moments of enlightenment for you to analyze and build future decisions and actions from, using everything you've learned.

Exercise 39: YOUR DECISIONS

Using the paper from Exercise 38, label the center column *Decisions,* and write down what decision you want to make regarding your moments of enlightenment.

Exercise 40: YOUR SUSTAINED ACTION

Using the paper from Exercise 39, label the right column *Sustained Actions,* and write down what sustained action you will have to do in order to change.

THE TOOLS AS APPLIED TO THIS BOOK

1. WHAT do I want to achieve?

- Primary Goal: I want to write a nonfiction book showing readers how to use Green Beret tactics and techniques to conquer fear and succeed.
- Subordinate goals and alignment (partial list):
- Break the entire concept down into easy-to-use tools. (This subordinate goal was developed after the first draft, when readers found the entire *Who Dares Wins* concept overwhelming in its entirety).
- Group the tools into three areas.
- Use examples so readers can understand.
- Give exercises so readers can apply templates to their lives.
- Coordinate the book with seminars, keynotes, and workshops (possible conflict here in that the book has to stand on its own without my presence as a speaker).

- Market the book.
- Redesign website to support the book.
  (There are many more subordinate goals, but this gives you an idea of how primary and subordinate goals work—and also how you have to look for present or potential conflict.)

2. WHY do I want to achieve my goal?

- I want to write *Who Dares Wins* because I believe the tactics and techniques of Special Forces can be applied to all individuals and make their lives better.
- Instead of throwing the entire concept at readers at once, I'll give it to them piecemeal, starting with the simplest area, WINS, and build on that.
- Instead of expecting readers to change their entire lives right away, I want to start small, so as not to overwhelm readers and cause them to quit.

3. WHERE do I want to achieve my goal?

- I am writing this book while also producing two novels, so I have to factor that into my scheduling and make sure I make my deadlines.
- For book dissection, I looked at numerous self-help, psychology, economic, philosophical, and historical books and examined their information and structure.
- For further research, I examined the many different paths to change and success that experts propose and compared them against the proven formula we use in Special Forces.
- In the bookstore, there are numerous self-help books. However, most of them are either theoretical, with few

practical applications, or so focused that they ignore the integration of all aspects of a person's life.

- In the larger environmental picture, this book is coming at the right time: the economy is in bad straits, there have been several large natural disasters, the country is at war, and people are feeling less confident than ever. This book fills a need.

4. Understand your CHARACTER and that of others.

- Profiling my habits, I discovered that I tend to do too much—to put too much information out there. In editing this book, I have constantly been cutting away material to try to focus the program as much as possible.
- I am an INFJ (author) according to the Myers-Briggs. Looking at the opposite character type to that, the ESTP (promoter), I realize I am weak in my ability to market this book and the *Who Dares Wins* program. I need to work with others who have experience in marketing and sales to compensate for this weakness. I also need to get out of my comfort zone and into my courage zone in this area.

5. What is CHANGE and how do you do it?

- The original draft of this book was 116,000 words. What you're reading is about 45,000. Remember earlier when I said one of the character traits I figured out was I tended to put out too much information? I changed. I cut and I cut and I cut to make this as straightforward as possible.
- I focused on individual improvement and team-building when I first wrote this book. It got to a point where I was

going in two directions at once. I had a moment of enlightenment and realized it would be confusing. After discussing it with my literary agent and getting input from others, I made a decision to focus the first book in this series on the individual. This was also based on the reality that individuals are the building blocks of teams. I then spent a considerable amount of time rewriting in order to achieve that goal.

6. How do you build COURAGE to change?

- This book is an example of catastrophe planning, and it is a parallel to my fiction writing career. The reality is that the fiction market is fickle. I began *Who Dares Wins* as a backup plan to my fiction writing and because I enjoy teaching.

7. COMMUNICATE your change to the world.

- You're holding it. In the written form.
- I also do keynotes, workshops, consulting, and seminars based on *Who Dares Wins* in which I combine this written form with oral communication.
- I constantly reevaluate and adjust these based on feedback from the audience and readers.

8. Take COMMAND of your change.

- I am responsible for everything in this book.
- While others are assisting me in marketing this book, the ultimate responsibility for it lies with me.

9. COMPLETE the Circle of Success and change.

- This book is about conquering fear and succeeding. This requires integration of many different aspects in a person's life. I've broken it down into three areas, with three tools in each, laid out a step-by-step plan, and then pulled it all together with the Circle of Success. The entire plan is laid out in Appendix A.

- This book breaks some of the rules for this genre. It covers more ground and is more complex than most. I think that's important, and I made that decision consciously because I wanted to present a complete plan for all aspects of a person's life, not just one specialized area standing alone. I take responsibility for the success or failure of that approach.

WHO DARES WINS:

BUILDING THE WINNING A-TEAM

A winning team is built with confident, successful individuals. This book is the first step in building a successful team. To build a winning A-Team, take all the tools in this book that are oriented inward, toward the individual, and turn them outward, toward the team.

When you walk around Ft. Bragg, you can tell who Special Forces are from a distance, before seeing their green berets or their patches. They stand out. They exude an air of confidence.

Why are they so confident? Training. No other soldier prepares like a Special Forces soldier. And what makes Special Forces teams so confident when they go on a mission? Preparation. No other unit in the Army prepares like a Special Forces team for a mission. And every member knows this.

On two levels—personal and mission-specific—*preparation* is the key.

The core of my approach for *Who Dares Wins* for teams/organizations is to cover in detail the flow of preparation that the Special Forces utilizes. It's not about the "mission" when I apply this to the civilian world, because the people I'm talking to are the experts at their mission, whether it be sales, IT, sports, educators. Where I can help is to show them the Special Forces way to prepare.

There is a specific flow:

1. MISSION TASKING

What: Write the goal in one sentence with one action verb. The clearly stated goals equal the standard for evaluation.

2. THE COMMANDER'S INTENT

Why: Know why the goal is to be achieved. This allows for innovation and improves motivation.

3. MISSION CONCEPT BRIEFING

Communicate: The team communicates back to the commander to ensure the team is on target for the right mission and to explore options for mission accomplishment. Begin support planning. Rule out options that are not feasible or cannot be supported.

4. ISOLATION AND MISSION PLANNING

Where: If an Area Study is not done, prepare one.

Use Standing Operation Procedures to codify actions, set standards, save time, and allow redundancy in the team.

Use the CARVER formula to analyze the problem and pick the best possible course of action.

Courage: Use catastrophe and worst-case planning to reduce anxiety and fear, and allow team members to focus their energies on success.

5. REHEARSALS

Character, Courage, and Change: Ensure priority of responsibilities and prepare for action.

6. THE SPECIAL FORCES BRIEF-BACK

Communicate: Make sure all coordination throughout the organization is completed and ready, and ensure all the support is in place.

Command: Get the commanders' approval for the mission, or be sent back to replan.

7. COMPLETE THE MISSION

To make it interesting and exciting, I use a real mission that my team conducted to show how each of these elements were used. I guarantee that even using part of the Special Forces way to prepare—either for an overall goal or for a specific task—will increase an organization/team's efficiency.

I can prepare an overview of Special Operations strategies for building your winning A-Team that will serve as a template; keynotes tailored to any of the nine tools in *Who Dares Wins*; or an inspirational keynote on the history of Special Operations Forces with lessons that your organization/team can use.

I can give a one-day intensive seminar that will focus on team leaders, introducing them in detail to the *Who Dares Wins* concept, the three problem areas, and the Special Operations solutions.

After observing your team in action, I will give a written and oral After Action Review with strategic and tactical solutions.

I help organizations build winning teams based on the most successful team in the world: the Special Forces A-Team. I guarantee that using even part of the *Who Dares Wins* concept will increase an organization/team's efficiency. So if you are part of a team, do you *dare* to win?

ABOUT THE AUTHOR

Bob Mayer is the best-selling author of more than thirty-eight books. He is a West Point graduate and has served in the infantry and in Special Forces (Green Berets)—commanding an A-Team and as a Special Forces battalion operations officer. Mayer was an instructor at the JFK Special Warfare Center and School at Fort Bragg. Bob earned an M.A. in education.

Mayer's books have hit the *New York Times*, *Wall Street Journal*, *Publishers Weekly*, *USA Today*, and other best-seller lists. He has appeared on local cable news channels around the country as well as on PBS, NPR, and the Discovery Military Channel—and in *USA Today*, the *Wall Street Journal*, and *Army Times*, among other publications—as an expert consultant.

Mayer is an honor graduate of the Combined Arms Services Staff School, the Infantry Office Basic and Advanced courses, the Special Forces Qualification Course, the Special Warfare Center Instructor Training Course, and the Danish Royal Navy Fromandkorpset School. He is master parachutist/jumpmaster-qualified, earned a black belt while living in the Orient, and has taught martial arts. He's spoken before more than five hundred groups and organizations, ranging from SWAT teams, IT teams in Silicon Valley, and the CIA to the University of Georgia, Romance Writers of America, and the Maui Writers Conference. He mixes practical Special Operations strategies with the vision of an artist.